New Covenant Salvation

G. R. Blair

For my brothers,
Jonny and Chris.

With thanks to my elders
in the Lord.

Foreword

When attempting to explain what New Covenant Salvation is, I have come to realise that terms such as 'sin', 'the fall', 'repentance', 'redemption' and even 'the gospel' are not as readily understood as they may, perhaps, have been understood in previous generations. There are probably a myriad of reasons for that, but the most basic one, perhaps, is that fewer people born today are growing up under the traditional teachings of the various Christian denominations. It may also be the case that fewer of those Christian denominations are teaching the gospel in all of its fullness.

It may also be the case that certain truths about the gospel have been watered down, or even lost.

Before talking about New Covenant Salvation, therefore, it is necessary to go back to fundamental truths about God, Himself, and about the original creation, the origin of sin, the fall, the consequences of the fall, repentance, redemption and everlasting life. Basic foundational truths that are salient to the teaching of New Covenant Salvation cannot now be taken for granted.

However, I would guard against forming the truth, as we may now see it, into an unalterable mould. God gave revelation in the beginning, as seen in Genesis, but He unfolded greater and deeper revelation as time went on, as can be seen in the unfolding of the scriptures. God also leads us into deeper revelation of the truth, as we continue to walk with Him, and we are each at different stages in our respective walks with God. We must be prepared, therefore, to receive further revelation from God and to patiently bear with one another.

We must also remember that learning everything about God is not our primary goal, but that our primary goal is truly to know and truly to love our Lord.

This book is intentionally short. It has primarily been written for the benefit of those who already know the Lord. However, it may also be useful to those who are genuinely seeking to know the Lord for the first time.

I am not attempting to say anything new and I am not presenting two sides of an argument. I am also not trying to form a fully-fledged theological framework for others to follow, as each of us must follow the Lord. I am only sharing the truths of New Covenant Salvation that have been revealed to me and to others.

I hope that it may be an aid to you, in your own walk with the Lord.

G. R. Blair

Contents

Chapter 1

The Invisible God

"For there are three that bear record in heaven, the Father, the Word, and the Holy Ghost: and these three are one."
(KJV 1 John 5:7)

"Before the mountains were brought forth, Or ever Thou hadst formed the earth and the world, Even from everlasting to everlasting, Thou art God."
(KJV Psalm 90:2)

Even before there was any space, or time, or matter there was God. God does not require space in which to live. He exists outside of time and He is not composed of matter.

God is Spirit and He precedes space, time and matter.

It is an understatement to say that it is difficult to imagine there being no space, or time, or matter. Even with the greatest of mental gymnastics, it is an extremely difficult concept for us to fathom.

It is similarly difficult for us to imagine ourselves as being non-existent; with no consciousness and with no ability to even think (i.e. absolute nothingness). What would absolute nothingness entail and how could anything ever come into being from absolute nothingness?

9

The Palmist eloquently states that, "Even from everlasting to everlasting, Thou art God" (KJV Psalm 90:2). Before the existence of space, or time, or matter, God simply was.

Consciousness, therefore, preceded the creation of the universe.

[As an aside, the acceptance, or denial, of the above statement profoundly shapes how each person views the world around them (i.e. their worldview), but it is universally accepted among the saints of God. For those who do not accept this statement, they must find a credible cause for the existence of the universe around them. Generally speaking, this creates a schism of worldviews between those who believe in a creator God and those who do not. The acceptance of either of these worldviews (or other possible worldviews) requires faith on the part of the believer, based on evidence.]

God has no beginning and He has no end. In a world where subjective truth is prevalent, God alone remains the great objective truth. Indeed, if all of space and time and matter were to be brought to nothing, only God would remain (together, of course, with any spirits that God had already breathed into being). Everything else is temporal in nature. Nothing else in all of existence is eternal. God simply is and ever will be.

God alone, being Spirit, is the ultimate truth and reality; not space, or time, or matter.

Before the existence of space, or time, or matter, God was. The opening verse of scripture states it more succinctly by declaring, "In the beginning God..." (KJV Genesis 1:1). Before anything else was, God was. The original word used for God in this passage is 'Elohim' and it occurs approximately 2,500 times in the scriptures. In the original language, the word 'Elohim' is the plural word for 'Eloah' and 'Eloah' occurs 56 times in the scriptures.

Whereas the word 'Eloah' refers to God in the singular (i.e. the one Supreme Being), the plural word 'Elohim' refers to the trinity of God acting in unity, or the trinity of God acting as One. This is, in fact, the earliest implicit reference in scripture to God the Father, God the Word and God the Holy Spirit and those names for God are fully expounded as the scriptures unfold.

We can see then that God the Father, God the Word and God the Holy Spirit are eternal. They exist outside of space and time and matter. They had no beginning and they will have no end. They, being Spirit, are the great objective truth and reality of existence. They are uncreated. They are something completely 'other than' the created world and the created universe around us.

We also see in Exodus 3:14 that God refers to Himself as, "I Am that I Am." This is a peculiar expression when it is translated into the English language. The thrust of the expression is not only that, "I Am", but that, "I continue to be and will be what I continue to be and will be," or, "I that ever will be," or, "the Ever-existing One." The simple truth is that God always has been and always will be and that He does not change.

Objective truth does not change.

I have said above that God is Spirit and that God is the ultimate truth and reality. Scripture also expressly reveals to us that, "God is love," (KJV 1 John 4:8) and that He is, "perfect" (KJV Matthew 5:48). The nature of

God is love and all that He does is done perfectly in love.

Love, therefore, is also the ultimate truth and reality.

God the Father, God the Word and God the Holy Spirit have known perfect loving fellowship with one another and they will continue to know perfect loving fellowship with one another for all eternity.

God is a conscious Being and He is a personal Being. He is perfect in love, in grace, in faith, in truth, in justice, in mercy, in compassion, in wisdom, in understanding, in counsel, in strength, in knowledge and in all other things. That is His nature. Not a single thought rises up in one Person of the Godhead that is not in perfect harmony and agreement with the other Persons of the Godhead.

God is One and He acts as One and He does so perfectly, in love.

[As an aside, God, as revealed in the scriptures, is the greatest conceivable Being that could possibly be. He is not a God of chaos, or of confusion. He consciously created a functioning universe, together with all that is in it, for a purpose. Is it any wonder, therefore, that the universe functions according to precise physical, biological, chemical and mathematical laws that we are able to observe?]

In our human relationships, we may often find that we put our own self-interests above the interests of others, or we may prefer one person above another. That is human nature. However, within the Godhead, there exists none of the self-serving that is universal to human nature. Each Person in the Godhead is continually giving of themselves to the other Persons in the

12

Godhead, without holding anything back. This is done in perfect trust and in perfect love and they have ever been doing so, from everlasting to everlasting. This is perfect love and it is sacrificial in nature.

Such love cannot be found outside of God.

This is what the Greeks described as 'agape' love, which is the very love of God. It is entirely separate from what the Greeks described as 'phileo' love, which is the affectionate love that exists naturally in man.

God is also entirely self-sufficient and it was never the case that He 'needed' to create anything. However, God did create. Forgive me for framing it in human terms, but a 'thought' arose in the heart of God the Father to create. The Father made His will known to the Word of God. In faith, the Word spoke out the will of the Father. The Holy Spirit, being in perfect agreement with the Father and with the Word, caused the will of the Father to be done.

All things, therefore, are of the Father, by the Word, through the Holy Spirit.

They function in perfect harmony, as One.

God is Spirit and He is, therefore, invisible (KJV Colossians 1:15). Indeed, the Apostle John confirmed that, "No man hath seen God at any time" (KJV 1 John 4:12). Part of the reason for God creating, therefore, was that He would make Himself known in, and by, His creation.

God revealed Himself to His creation.

Chapter 2

God Begins To Make Himself Known

"Of old hast Thou laid the foundations of the earth: And the heavens are the work of Thy hands. They shall perish, but Thou shalt endure: Yea, all of them shall wax old like a garment; As a vesture shalt Thou change them, And they shall be changed: But Thou art the same, And Thy years shall have no end."
(KJV Psalm 102:25-27)

"The heavens declare (i.e. are continually declaring) the glory of God and the firmament sheweth (i.e. is continually showing) His handiwork."
(KJV Psalm 19:1)

The point was perhaps laboured, but in Chapter 1 it was emphasised that God did not have a beginning and that He will not have an end. He is from everlasting to everlasting. The present chapter deals with how God, who is invisible, began to make Himself known in, and by, His creation, which certainly did have a beginning.

It is fitting that the first verses of scripture are also some of the most beautiful verses in all of scripture:-

"In the beginning (i.e. the beginning of the creation) God (that is 'Elohim', being plural) created (i.e. created out of

14

absolutely nothing) the heaven[s] (the original word for 'heaven' is plural) and the earth. And the earth was without form and void; and darkness was upon the face of the deep. And the Spirit of God moved (i.e. was continually moving) upon the face of the waters." (KJV Genesis 1:1-2)

[As a little aside, it is poignant to note that when the earth was made, having yet no life upon it, the Spirit of God was continually moving upon the face of the waters. This is not simply a beautiful image of the Holy Spirit and His intimate care of the earth. It preluded the coming forth of life upon the earth (which had no life in it), which in turn acted as a foreshadowing of the Holy Spirit coming upon the virgin Mary (to conceive the life of Christ within her). It also foreshadowed the Holy Spirit moving upon the heart of man, both corporately and individually.]

One thing should be made clear at this point. God is a faith being. When God speaks, things simply happen. He acts by His own faith, which is the very faith of God. When God speaks creation into being, therefore, He does not speak *hoping* that it will occur. Rather, He speaks *knowing* that it will occur.

It comes as no surprise then, that when God says, "Let there be light," (KJV Genesis 1:3) on day one of creation, light must come forth. God precedes His creation and He is sovereign within His creation.

God is the sole author of creation.

The rest of the creation account that is detailed in Genesis 1:3-31 should not, therefore, come as any

15

surprise to us. God spoke and the firmament was created (i.e. created out of existing materials), dividing the waters from the waters (day two of creation). God spoke and dry land came forth (day three of creation) and the vegetation of the earth came forth, thereafter, when God watered the earth (Genesis 2:4-6). God spoke and the sun, the moon and the stars were brought forth (day four of creation). God spoke and the birds of the air and the creatures of the sea were brought forth (day five of creation). God spoke and the land animals were brought forth and mankind was formed and made (day six of creation). God looked at what He had created and declared that it was, "very good," (KJV Genesis 1:31) before resting from his work on the seventh day.

It should be made clear that when God declares that the creation is very good, He means that it is, in fact, perfect, for God does not do imperfect work.

What then can we say about the creation?

God the Father purposed in His heart to create and He made His will known to the Word of God. The Word of God, in faith, spoke out that which was in the heart of the Father. The Holy Spirit, being in perfect agreement with the Father and with the Word, caused the creation to be.

All things are of the Father, by the Word, through the Holy Spirit and all things were created perfectly.

God, who is Spirit and who is invisible, spoke creation into being, but why? The Apostle Paul, when writing to the Romans, gives a clear answer:-

> "…that which may be known of God is
> manifest in (or among) them (i.e. man);
> for God hath shewed it unto them (i.e. to

mankind and the various powers and principalities). For the invisible things of Him (i.e. God) from the creation of the world are clearly seen, being understood by the things that are made, even His (i.e. God's) eternal power and Godhead (or divinity)." (KJV Romans 1:19-20)

God created the heavens and the earth for man and for the various powers and principalities. God created a habitation for man, so that He could create man and reveal Himself to man (more on this in Chapter 3).

What Paul is really saying above is that when man looks upon the earth (and all that is in the earth) and looks upon the sun, the moon and the stars, he (i.e. man) is really looking at the handiwork of God. Man should be glorifying God, therefore, simply from observing what he sees in the creation around him.

The creation itself witnesses to the glory of God, so that all of mankind is left without excuse for believing whether God is true, or not. Of course, the powers and principalities that are looking on (i.e. the angels, Satan and Satan's fallen angels) can also see the glory of God in the creation. The creation also serves, therefore, as a witness against them.

The Apostle John also left us in no doubt as to how the universe came to be when he wrote:-

"In the beginning was the Word, and the Word was with God, and the Word was God. The same was in the beginning with God. All things were made (i.e. came into being) by Him; and without

17

Him was not anything made that was made." (KJV John 1:1-3)

It is no wonder that the Psalmist also declares that, "The earth is full of the goodness of the LORD," (KJV Psalm 33:5) and, "O LORD, how manifold are Thy works! In wisdom hast thou made them all: The earth is full of Thy riches" (KJV Psalm 104:24). [The word 'LORD' here is simply a translation of 'Jehovah', which, when translated, means He that is, and that was, and that is to come.]

There is far too much to quote here verbatim, but for the reader who is genuinely interested in seeing the poetical beauty of what God has done in creation, I would strongly recommend that you read all of Job 38 and 39, so that God, Himself, may speak to you out of the whirlwind.

Psalm 104 may also be of interest to the reader regarding the creation.

What then can we say?

God is from everlasting to everlasting. God is Spirit, God is love and God is perfect. All that God does is done perfectly in love. It cannot be otherwise. Being invisible, God spoke creation into being. That creation was made perfectly and it was made to declare the glory of God.

It is extremely difficult for us to imagine what that perfect creation was really like and we could speculate endlessly about it. The fact that it was created for man, however, should humble each and every one of us.

It is to man whom we now turn.

Chapter 3

Man Created In The Image Of God

"...For I have created (i.e. called into being out of nothing) him (i.e. man) for My glory, I have formed (i.e. fashioned into an appointed form) him; yea, I have made (i.e. out of pre-existing material) him."
(KJV Isaiah 43:7)

The creation of the heavens and the earth was glorious, in and of itself, and they continue to declare the glory of God. Man was also created for the glory of God. However, we see something much more intimate in the creation of man. For the first time in all of creation (including the creation of the angels), we see a creature in which the very glory of God was to be manifested.

Whereas the creation was made to be the habitation of man, man was made to be the habitation of God.

In addition to Isaiah 43:7, quoted above, the scriptures describe the creation of man as follows:-

"And God (i.e. 'Elohim', being plural) said, 'Let us (i.e. plural) make man (i.e. 'ahdahm') in our image (the word for image being singular), after our own likeness (the word for likeness also being

singular); and let him have dominion.'"
(KJV Genesis 1:26)

"So God (i.e. 'Elohim', being plural)
created man (i.e. 'ahdahm') in His image,
in the image of God created He him;
male and female created He them." (KJV
Genesis 1:27)

In all of creation, no other being is described as being made in the image of God, except man. There was something within man that enabled him to seek after God and to have fellowship with God.

Moreover, dominion of the earth was entrusted to man. Man was created, therefore, to possess and to have stewardship of the earth and all that was therein.

It should be emphasised that man's body was not created out of nothing. Rather, man's body was formed (i.e. fashioned into an appointed form) and made (i.e. out of pre-existing material):-

"And the LORD God (i.e. 'Jehovah',
'Elohim', being plural) formed man (i.e.
'ahdahm') of the dust of the ground (i.e.
of the earth; hence earthy), and breathed
into his nostrils the breath of life (i.e.
plural); and man (i.e. 'ahdahm') became
a living soul." (KJV Genesis 2:7)

Whereas God spoke and the various creatures of the earth came into being, God (being Spirit) breathed spirit into the body of man and man became a living soul. Job was able to declare, therefore, that in God's, "hand is the soul of every living thing, and the breath of all mankind" (KJV Job 12:10). Likewise, Zechariah saw that it is God who, "formeth the spirit of man within him" (KJV Zechariah 12:10). It was Paul, however, in his first letter to the Thessalonians, who emphasised what man actually is:-

> "And the very God of peace sanctify you wholly; and your whole (i.e. your entire) spirit and soul and body be preserved blameless unto the coming of our Lord Jesus Christ." (KJV 1 Thessalonians 5:23)

Adam had a body and, when God breathed spirit into him, Adam became a living soul. Man, therefore, has a *spirit*, a *soul* and a *body*.

Adam was spiritually alive and without sin and innocent. If we recall what is said in Genesis 1:31, Adam was created perfectly as the first man. How then was Adam (and his progeny) to function?

Let us look briefly at the personal spirit within a man.

Adam had his own individual spirit (as we all have), which was personal to him (as our own individual spirit is personal to each of us). God is Spirit and He is the Father of all spirits. God, therefore, fathered Adam's spirit (i.e. God breathed Adam's spirit into him).

Adam was to commune with God, in spirit, and was to have perfect and unbroken fellowship with God. Adam was speaking directly with God, therefore, and was hearing God, unhindered. The deep things within

Adam (i.e. in his spirit) were able to call out to the deep things of God and vice versa (Psalm 42:7).

Another function of the personal spirit within a man is intuition. Being in perfect fellowship with God, God could reveal all things into Adam's spirit (i.e. direct revelation from God). Adam was not, therefore, working out everything for himself intellectually. Rather, Adam was receiving everything directly from God by revelation because, ultimately, it is God who leads us into all truth (John 16:13).

The conscience is also a function of the personal spirit within a man. Provided the conscience is pure, we are made aware (i.e. become pricked) in spirit if something is wrong. This helps to ensure that perfect fellowship with God remains unbroken. It is, of course, possible for the conscience within a man to be damaged so that it no longer functions as it ought to, but that is not the focus of this chapter.

Let us also look briefly at the human soul.

The human soul is essentially the natural life of a man and it was formed to be in subjection to the personal spirit within a man. Our souls are primarily composed of our minds, our wills and our emotions (i.e. basic human functions), but there may, of course, be other aspects to our souls.

Adam was in perfect spiritual fellowship with God. He was also receiving revelation directly from God, in his spirit. The deep things of God were being made known to him. The natural outworking of such revelation was that his mind would, in turn, understand what God had said so that he could glorify God.

Similarly, knowing that God had spoken to him, Adam could freely exercise his will to determine to believe God and to follow God. The will of man was, therefore, to be in perfect subjection to God's own will. In so doing, the very emotions of man's soul were to be kept in perfect subjection to his will, so that they could develop along the line that God had intended (i.e. not along the line of 'self').

Adam also had a human body. It was formed and made from the dust of the earth and was a body of flesh. However, it was not formed and made as a body of sin, like we have. Rather, Adam's body was perfectly formed and made with the intention that it would become the temple of the living God. It was not, therefore, an instrument of sin.

What then do we see?

God is Spirit and is the Father of all spirits. The personal spirit within man was to have pre-eminence over the soul of man, which, in turn, was to have pre-eminence over the body of man. Adam was to receive absolutely everything from God, in his spirit, to the end that his soul would develop (or grow up) into Godliness and show forth the glory of God in his body, which was intended to be (or to become) the very temple of the living God.

It was intended that God was to sit upon the throne of the heart of man, therefore, wherein abides the spirit and the soul of man, so that the whole thrust of man was to serve God.

The personal spirit within man was to be in complete subjection to God. The soul within man was to be in complete subjection to the personal spirit within man and the body of man was to be in complete subjection to the soul within man.

Everything within man was set in order by God.

As the first man, therefore, Adam was placed upon the earth to grow up into all Godliness and to show forth the glory of God upon the earth, which had been given to Adam as his possession.

How then did it all go so wrong?

Chapter 4

The Fall Of Man

"Of every tree of the garden thou mayest freely eat; but of the tree of the knowledge of good and evil, thou shalt not eat of it: for in the day that thou eatest thereof thou shalt surely die."
(KJV Genesis 2:16-17)

God created man and placed him in the Garden of Eden, in order to dress it and to keep it. God later formed Eve, out of Adam, so that Adam had a companion upon the earth that was perfectly meet, or perfectly suitable, for him.

It is difficult for us to comprehend just how wonderful creation would have been at that time, or for how long Adam and Eve lived in Eden to enjoy that wonderful creation. It could have been a day, a week, a month, a year, a decade, a century, a millennium etc.

We simply do not know, but God knows.

However, there was one caveat to living in the Garden of Eden. God had given one law to Adam that both he and Eve were to obey:-

"And the LORD God (i.e. 'Jehovah', 'Elohim') commanded the man (i.e. 'ahdahm'), saying, 'Of every tree of the garden thou mayest freely eat; but of the tree of the knowledge of good and evil,

thou shalt not eat of it: for in the day that
thou eatest thereof thou shalt surely die.'"
(KJV Genesis 2:16-17)

We saw in Chapter 2 that God is a faith being.
By giving Adam one law to follow, God was giving
Adam the opportunity to relate to Him by faith. The just
live by faith (Habakkuk 2:4) and if Adam and Eve
believed God and obeyed that one law, by faith, they
would have remained just in the eyes of God.

However, most of us will be familiar with what
actually did occur:-

> "And the serpent (i.e. Satan, the
> adversary) said unto the woman (i.e.
> Eve), 'Ye shall not surely die: for God
> doth know that in the day ye eat thereof,
> then your eyes shall be opened, and ye
> shall be as gods (or perhaps, as God)
> knowing good and evil.'" (KJV Genesis
> 3:4-5)

[As an aside, it was originally Satan, of course, in
his pride, who believed that he could be as God and
Satan's fall preceded the fall of mankind because of that
false belief.]

We saw in Chapter 3 how God was to sit upon
the throne of the heart of man. Man's personal spirit
was to be in fellowship with, and in subjection to, God.
In turn, man's soul was to be in subjection to his
personal spirit and his body was to be in subjection to
his soul. That was the order that was ordained by God
for man. However, what we see here is Satan speaking,

26

not into the personal spirit of man, as God does, but, rather, to the soul of man.

Satan is not omniscient. Only God is omniscient. God knows every single thought of man and can reveal truth directly into the personal spirit within a man. Satan does not know the thoughts of man and he cannot speak directly into the personal spirit within a man, but he does know the commandments, or laws, that God has given to man to obey.

Obedience starts with believing what God has said is true. The surest way for man to show God that he does not believe God is for man to disobey God. Any decision to disobey God can only come from within the soul of man (i.e. man's mind and will).

Satan tempted man, therefore, along the line of his soul.

Using her mind to dwell upon what Satan had said to her, rather than believing what God had said was true, Eve looked at the fruit of the tree of the knowledge of good and evil and saw that it was pleasant to the eyes, that it was good for food and that it was to be desired to make one wise. This is simply a reflection of the lust of the eyes, the lust of the flesh and the pride of life, as identified by the Apostle John:-

> "Love not the world, neither the things that are in the world. If any man love[s] the world, the love of the Father is not in him. For all that is in the world, the lust of the flesh, and the lust of the eyes, and the pride of life, is not of the Father, but is of the world. And the world passeth away, and the lust thereof: but he that

doeth the will of God abideth for ever."
(KJV 1 John 2:15-17)

Rather than believing God and doing what God had said, Eve, being deceived in her soul, gave in to Satan's temptation and ate of the tree of the knowledge of good and evil. Eve also gave of the fruit to Adam and Adam willingly chose to eat of it.

As the Apostle Paul clarified in his first letter to Timothy (1 Timothy 2:14), Adam was not actually deceived. Rather, Eve was deceived and was in the transgression. The inference may be that Adam saw Eve (who was the only creature that was formed to be perfectly suitable for Adam) in her fallen state and he willingly chose to follow her into that fallen state, rather than risk losing her altogether.

In any event, Adam also transgressed the law and sinned against God:-

> "And the eyes of both of them were opened...and they heard the voice of the LORD God (i.e. 'Jehovah', 'Elohim') ...and Adam and his wife hid themselves from the presence of the LORD God."
> (KJV Genesis 3:7-8)

Adam explained to God that he was hiding because he was afraid. Fear was not something that Adam, or Eve, had previously experienced. Fear was a product of sin and, because of that sin, God expelled Adam and Eve from the Garden of Eden, lest they would also eat of the tree of life and live forever in their fallen state.

Moreover, in giving way to Satan, Adam also surrendered possession of the earth to Satan. However, even at that time, God promised a remedy:-

"And the LORD God (i.e. 'Jehovah', 'Elohim') said unto the serpent, 'Because thou hast done this...I will put enmity (i.e. active opposition) between thee and the woman, and between thy seed and her seed; it shall bruise thy head (accomplished by Christ on the cross), and thou shalt bruise his heel (a picture of Christ dying on the cross and, perhaps, a picture of Satan opposing the Church, as the feet of Christ upon the earth).'" (KJV Genesis 3:14-15)

What then do we see?

Man did not believe God and when he ate of the tree of the knowledge of good and evil he sinned. That sin broke man's perfect spiritual fellowship with God and, as such, man died spiritually (physical death also followed). Rather than receiving everything from God, in spirit, man now had to use his mind and his will (i.e. the natural capacities of his fleshly soul) to determine, himself, what was good and what was evil.

Man's soul gained pre-eminence, therefore, over his personal spirit.

In a sense, man did become his own god, but 'self' became his master. 'Self' now sat upon the throne of man's heart and not God. Man became a slave to 'self' and a slave to the law of sin and death that was now at work within him (more on this later).

Man's very nature had changed.

Man's soul would not now grow up into Godliness, as God had originally intended. Rather, man's soul would now grow up in accordance with the lust of his eyes, the lust of his flesh and the pride of life.

Ultimately, man's soul would crave the things of the flesh, the things of the world and even the things of Satan. In time, his body would even obtain pre-eminence over his soul (i.e. over his will to choose) and the order that God had ordained for man would be turned completely upside down.

Man's soul would, thereafter, grow up into all Godlessness.

Chapter 5

The Heart Of Man

"For the eyes of the LORD (i.e. 'Jehovah') run to and fro throughout the whole earth, to shew himself (i.e. God) strong in the behalf of them (i.e. man) whose heart is perfect toward him (i.e. God)."
(2 Chronicles 16:9)

"It is a people that do err in their heart, And they have not known My ways."
(KJV Psalm 95:10)

"...out of the heart of men proceed evil thoughts...and all these evil things come from within and defile the man..."
(KJV Matthew 7:20-23)

The term 'The Fall' is not found in the scriptures, but it is the term that is normally used when referring to Adam sinning in the Garden of Eden and breaking perfect spiritual fellowship with God, as we saw in Chapter 4.

We saw what Adam was formed to be in Chapter 3. We will take some time now to look at what man became, ultimately, after The Fall.

Adam sinned and all of his progeny are born with that same sinful nature because the law of sin and death is at work in all of Adam's progeny. The Apostle Paul declared that, "all have sinned, and come short (or fall short) of the glory of God" (KJV Romans 3:23). What Adam did, therefore, affected the entire human race.

The nature of man was fundamentally altered.

Man has a spirit, a soul and a body and it was originally intended that God was to be seated upon the throne of man's heart. Man was supposed to give himself over to God, in humility; spirit, soul and body (i.e. wholeheartedly). However, Adam's sin, in the Garden of Eden, dethroned God from the heart of man (that is, if God had ever truly been established upon the throne of man's heart to begin with) and established man's sinful self-nature as the god of man's heart. Man became a slave to sin and a slave to self, which brought death.

The law of sin and death reigns in the heart of man, therefore, and this will be explained further in Chapter 6.

Man's personal spirit, which was to have the pre-eminence, was also displaced by his soul. Perfect spiritual fellowship with God had been broken and the communion that man was supposed to know with God was fundamentally tarnished. This is something that fallen man could never wholly re-establish by himself and, by and large, man did not want to re-establish perfect spiritual fellowship with God.

Similarly, the intuitive nature of man's spirit was impaired. Whereas man had known what it was to be aware of God's presence and to hear God and to speak with God, man was now on the pathway to becoming blind, deaf and mute to the things of God. Rather than receiving revelation from God, man strove to do things his own way.

Further, what Adam must have felt in his conscience at the time of The Fall is almost incomprehensible. Never before had Adam known what it was to disappoint God. The dulling of the conscience in Adam's progeny was to become all too clear, as the conscience of man became seared and insensitive to the correction of God.

Rather than receiving everything from God's hand, man became his own god, but 'self' became his master. Man had eaten of the tree of the knowledge of good and evil and man now had to work out everything for himself, in his own strength, as he thought best. It may surprise the reader, but this is something that God had never intended for man.

Man was now using his mind to pursue knowledge, rather than humbling himself and being taught by God. This is something that has been evident throughout the history of man, whereby the pursuit of knowledge and intelligence has practically been idolised and worshipped by man.

For example, education does, of course, have its place and, if we wish to excel in the world, we must learn knowledge in the way that the world teaches it. However, it remains the case that God is still willing to teach man, by revelation, if man is willing to humble himself before God and listen. If we wish to excel in the kingdom of God, therefore, we must humbly return to God and receive revelation from Him, rather than relying upon our own reasoning, our own thoughts and the countless opinions of man.

Man was also exercising his will after The Fall, but it was not being exercised under the will of God, or subject to the will of God. Rather, man's will was purposefully striving against the will of God. Man was working everything out for himself, in pride, for his own glory and not for God's glory.

Similarly, man's emotions were now being driven by 'self', be it self-indulgence, self-pity, self-centredness, self-loathing, self-serving etc. The list is virtually endless. Moreover, man's emotions were not in subjection to his will, so that the emotions of the 'self' life became the driving force behind the will of man.

Whereas man's body had originally been created to become the temple of the living God, this had become defiled by sin and became a body of sin, resulting in physical death. The cravings of the body (i.e. of the flesh) were now able to overcome the mind and the will of man, so that man's body could dictate a man's actions.

Man became a slave indeed!

Ultimately, however, man rejected God in his heart:-

> "...when they knew God, they glorified Him not as God, neither were thankful; but became vain in their imaginations, and their foolish heart was darkened. Professing themselves to be wise, they became fools, and changed the glory of the uncorruptable God into an image made like to corruptible man, and to birds, and fourfooted beasts, and creeping things. Wherefore God also gave them up to uncleanness through the lusts of their own hearts, to dishonour their bodies between themselves: who changed

the truth of God into a lie, and worshipped and served the creature more than the creator." (KJV Romans 1:21-24)

Man had been created in the image of God to the end that he would know God, in his spirit, so that his soul would develop up into all Godliness and his body would become the temple of the living God. However, man did not retain God in his knowledge. Instead, man pursued vain things in the pursuit of knowledge and in striving to be his own god. Rather than bearing the image of God, therefore, man became deaf, blind and mute to the things of God, just as the idols that he made (i.e. out of gold, silver, wood and stone etc.) were deaf, blind and mute.

Man could not attain to the glory for which God had created him, so man made his own gods and gave them glory instead.

It is no wonder that scripture records that, "The heart (i.e. of man) is deceitful above all things, and desperately wicked" (KJV Jeremiah 17:9). The heart of man lusts after the things of the flesh and the things of the world. It lusts after that which brings death and it cannot get enough of it. Rather than expressing the image of God, therefore, the heart of man expresses man's own fallen and depraved image.

Nevertheless, God has ever pleaded with man to return to Him.

"The fear of the LORD (i.e. 'Jehovah') is the beginning of knowledge, but fools despise wisdom and instruction" (KJV Proverbs 1:7). "Trust in the LORD with all thine heart; and lean not unto thine own understanding" (KJV Proverbs 3:5). "My son, give me thine heart and let thine eyes observe my ways" (KJV Proverbs 23:26). "Blessed are the poor (or humble) in spirit: for theirs is the kingdom of heaven" (KJV Matthew 5:3). "Blessed are the pure in heart, for they will see God" (KJV Matthew 5:8). It is no wonder, therefore, that King David cried out, "Create in me a clean heart, O God; and renew a right spirit within me" (KJV Psalm 51:10).

God, Himself, also rhetorically asked, "Have I any pleasure at all that the wicked should die? saith the LORD God (i.e. 'Jehovah', 'Elohim'): and not that he should return from his ways, and live?" (KJV Ezekiel 18:23).

The pleading of God's own heart was also beautifully expressed through the prophets, Joel and Jeremiah:-

> "Therefore also now, saith the LORD (i.e. 'Jehovah'), Turn ye even to Me with all your heart, And with fasting, and with weeping, and with mourning: And rend your heart, and not your garments, And turn unto the LORD your God (i.e. 'Jehovah', 'Elohim'): For He is gracious and merciful, slow to anger, and of great kindness, And repenteth Him of the evil." (KJV Joel 2:12-13)

> "Obey, I beseech thee, the voice of the LORD (i.e. 'Jehovah'), which I speak unto thee: so it shall be well unto thee, and thy soul shall live." (KJV Jeremiah 38:20)

36

Micah 6:8 essentially declares all that God requires of man:-

> "He (i.e. God) hath showed thee, O man, what is good; And what doth the LORD (i.e. 'Jehovah') require of thee, But to do justly, and to love mercy, And to walk humbly with thy God?" (KJV)

However, man, in his pride (i.e. akin to Satan), has rejected God to his hurt:-

> "And even as they did not like to retain God in their knowledge, God gave them over to a reprobate mind, to do those things which are not convenient; being filled with all unrighteousness, fornication, wickedness, covetousness, maliciousness; full of envy, murder, debate, deceit, malignity; whisperers, backbiters, haters of God, despiteful, proud, boasters, inventors of evil things, disobedient to parents, without understanding, covenantbreakers, without natural affection, implacable, unmerciful: who knowing the judgment of God, that they which commit such things are worthy of death, not only do the same, but have pleasure in them that do them." (KJV Romans 1:28-32)

We see, therefore, that the heart of man, after the fall, is not inherently good, or Godly. Rather, the heart of man, after the fall, is inherently evil and wicked.

What then is the natural outworking of the heart of man?

Chapter 6

The Law Of Sin And Death

"Wherefore, as by one man sin entered into the world, and death by sin; and so death passed upon all men, for that all have sinned."
(KJV Romans 5:12)

We have seen what man was created to be. We have also seen what man ultimately became after The Fall, but what is the natural outworking of the heart of man since The Fall?

In his transgression, Adam condemned all of mankind. Rather, Adam pre-destined the entire race of man to sin and death. We will take some time now to see the natural outworking of this law of sin and death in the heart of man.

As stated previously, what God has always asked of man is made plain in the scriptures:-

"He (i.e. God) hath showed thee, O man, what is good; And what doth the LORD (i.e. 'Jehovah') require of thee, But to do justly, and to love mercy, And to walk humbly with thy God?" (KJV Micah 6:8)

However, since The Fall, man has not walked humbly with God. Rather, man has deliberately walked in the pride of life. He has lifted up and exalted himself.

He has determined that he can live out his life apart from God.

Man has determined to do things his own way. It is rightly recorded in the scriptures, therefore, that, "his soul (i.e. man's soul) which is lifted up (i.e. is proud) is not upright in him" (KJV Habakkuk 2:4).

Let us now take a look at a few examples from scripture.

Within one generation from Adam, Cain and his brother, Abel, offered sacrifices to God. God was pleased with Abel's sacrifice (which was of the firstlings of his flock of sheep), but not Cain's (which was of the fruit of the ground). Abel offered a lamb, which may have pointed towards the Lamb of God laying down His life on the cross, whereas Cain offered the fruit of the ground and the ground had been cursed following Adam's sin in the Garden of Eden.

God was not pleased with Cain's sacrifice, yet He appealed to Cain by saying, "If thou doest well, shalt thou not be accepted? And if thou doest not well sin lieth at the door. And unto thee shall be his desire" (KJV Genesis 4:7).

Ultimately, we learn in Hebrews 11:4 that God was pleased with Abel's sacrifice because it was offered in faith and without faith it is impossible to please God (Hebrews 11:6). However, Cain's sacrifice was not offered in faith and God's judgment in the matter fully revealed the natural outworking of Cain's heart. Rather than humbling himself before God, "Cain rose up against Abel his brother, and slew him" (KJV Genesis 4:8).

Within one generation of Adam, the first murder in human history occurred.

When describing Satan, Jesus said that, "He was a murderer from the beginning, and abode not in the truth, because there is no truth in him" (KJV John 8:44). Satan had essentially murdered Adam and all of his progeny and that same murderous spirit had crept into the heart of man.

We also see a very clear picture in Cain and Abel. We see that there will be two different kinds of people upon the earth. There will be those who believe God and humble themselves before God and there will be those who do not believe God and who rebel against God.

From Adam to Noah (i.e. before the flood), there were approximately ten generations of man. With the exception of the righteous line of Seth (i.e. Adam's third son, from whom Enoch and Noah came), we see, perhaps, the greatest demonstration of the outworking of the law of sin and death in the heart of man in all of scripture. At that time, God looked upon the face of the whole earth and came to a truly sad and horrifying conclusion:-

> "...God saw that the wickedness of man was great in the earth, and that every imagination of the thoughts of his heart (i.e. man's heart) was only evil continually. And it repented the LORD (i.e. 'Jehovah') that he had made man on the earth, and it grieved him at his heart."
> (KJV Genesis 6:5-6)

Essentially, man proved to God exactly what fallen man is. Man's nature is inherently sinful, fleshly

41

and evil and, if left completely unchecked, man is (and will be) continually evil all of the time. It is nothing less than the natural outworking of the lust of the eyes, the lust of the flesh and the pride of life (i.e. the prideful thought within man that he is great and that he can do everything in his own strength, without God).

This is the natural outworking of the law of sin and death within man.

We may look at the world around us in our day (with all of our hindsight and advantages) and be appalled at the evil that we see within man today. Different examples will immediately spring to mind in each and every person. However, we can only wonder what it was like in the days of Noah when all that was in the heart of man was only evil, continually (i.e. in the heart of every single person upon the earth except Noah and, presumably, Noah's family).

God's judgment upon the earth in the days of Noah is striking and it should speak to us in our day:-

> "And the LORD said, 'My Spirit shall not always strive with man, for that he is also flesh...The end of all flesh is come before me; for the earth is filled with violence through them; and, behold, I will destroy them with the earth.'" (KJV Genesis 6:3 and 13)

God sent a flood upon the earth that destroyed man at that time, therefore, save Noah and his family because, "Noah found grace in the eyes of the LORD" (KJV Genesis 6:8). God was gracious towards Noah because, "Noah was a just man and perfect in his generations, and Noah walked (i.e. walked habitually) with God" (KJV Genesis 6:9).

How was Noah perfect in his generations before God? Noah, being a sinner, believed God, humbled himself before God and followed God.

Brevity only permits us to look at four other examples from scripture.

Within three generations of Noah (i.e. man's new start after the flood), Nimrod was born and, "he began to be a mighty one in the earth. He was a mighty hunter (a better translation may be 'a mighty rebel') before the LORD...and the beginning of his kingdom was Babel, and Elech, and Accad, and Calneh, in the land of Shinar" (KJV Genesis 10:8-10).

The whole earth was of one language at that time and they (i.e. man) determined to build a city and a tower (i.e. the tower of Babel) that would reach to heaven so that they could, "make a name," for themselves (KJV Genesis 11:4). This was nothing less than the prideful glorification of man and the image of man, rather than the glorification of God.

God quickly brought the building of the tower of Babel to an end by confusing the language of the people, who then dispersed across the face of the earth. It was at that time, perhaps, that the false religion(s) of Babel (i.e. the deification of Nimrod as a god, the worship of his wife, Semiramis, as the mother of god, and the worship of their son, Tammuz, as the son of god) also spread across the earth. For a deeper look at this subject, I would recommend reading a little book called 'The Principality and Power of Europe' that was written by Adrian Hilton.

God called Abraham (or Abram) in the same age as Nimrod and many truly wonderful things could be said of Abraham, especially as regards the picture of the righteousness by faith that was to come, apart from the law (as given to Moses). However, it was at the time of Abraham that God destroyed the cities of Sodom and Gomorrah with brimstone and fire from heaven because, "the cry of Sodom and Gomorrah [was] great, and because their sin [was] very grievous" (KJV Genesis 18:20).

This was because of the sins of the flesh to which the Apostle Paul refers in Romans 1:26-27. Here we see the fleshly body of man overcoming the soul of man, so that man becomes subject to affections that are contrary to nature. This again is the natural outworking of the law of sin and death in the heart of man, the end of which is death and the destruction of the flesh.

God later gave the law to Moses and to the children of Israel when they came out of Egypt. The law not only revealed God's own character, but it helped to identify what was utterly sinful in God's eyes. This should have resulted in the widespread humbling of hearts before God (and sometimes it did). However, the law was written in stone and not upon the fleshly tables of man's heart. The law did not, therefore, change the heart of man within him. Rather, man remained proud and hard against God.

Read the book of Judges (especially chapters 19-21) and you will realise that, even with the law, the heart of man remained desperately wicked. "In those days there was no king in Israel: every man did that which was right in his own eyes," (KJV Judges 21:25) rather than seeking God and the natural outworking of that disposition was often truly awful.

When the children of Israel subsequently asked God for a king (as the other nations of the earth had kings), God was displeased with them because God was their King. However, God gave them Saul to be king and, naturally speaking, Saul was a good choice as he was strong, but his heart wandered away from God. God chose David to be king, therefore, as David was a man after God's own heart (1 Samuel 13:14). God was gracious to David and he won the kingdom through much bloodshed, which is a picture of Christ winning the kingdom on the cross. David's son, Solomon, was able to reign in peace, therefore, as all of his enemies had already been defeated, which is a picture of Christ and His Church reigning in glory.

However, following Solomon's death, the kingdom split into two kingdoms, namely Israel and Judah. Thereafter, each kingdom entered into general decline (except in the days of Hezekiah and Josiah and other faithful kings) because they, by and large, turned away from God.

Ultimately, Israel was judged by God and was conquered by Assyria. Likewise, Judah was also judged by God and was conquered by Babylon. Examples of what the children of Israel were doing at that time are recorded in scripture:-

> "They (i.e. the children of Israel) have turned unto Me (i.e. God) the back, and not the face: though I taught them, rising up early and teaching them, yet they have not hearkened to receive instruction (i.e.

God sent His prophets to them). But they set their abominations (i.e. their idols) in the house, which is called by my name (i.e. the Temple), to defile it. And they built the high places of Baal (i.e. a pagan god), which are in the valley of the son of Hinnom, to cause their sons and their daughters to pass through the fire unto Molech (i.e. child sacrifice); which I commanded them not, neither came it into My mind, that they should do this abomination, to cause Judah to sin." (KJV Jeremiah 32:33-35)

It seems an incredible thing that man could conceive of doing evil that had never come into the mind of God.

Truly, man is left floundering without God seated upon the throne of his heart.

Chapter 7

God Promises A New Thing

"Eye hath not seen, Nor ear heard, Neither have entered into the heart of man, The things which God hath prepared for them that love Him."
(KJV 1 Corinthians 2:9 and Isaiah 64:4)

The law had been given by God to Moses, after the children of Israel had been delivered by God from the bondage of Egypt. By the law we mean the Ten Commandments, the sacrificial system, the levitical priesthood and a myriad of other supplemental rules, regulations and statutes that God gave to Moses, which Moses, thereafter, gave to the children of Israel to live by ("the Law").

This was the Old Covenant, whereby those who kept the Law would live by the Law (Leviticus 18:5) and the blood of animals was continually shed to cover the trespasses and the sins of the people.

The Law was given to the children of Israel and it completely distinguished them from all of the other nations on the earth. It helped to set them apart as God's chosen people. God was demonstrating to Satan and the powers and principalities that He was able to draw out, or raise up, His own peculiar people from among the fallen nations of the earth, over which Satan had possession and dominion.

God was creating a holy nation. He drew it out of Egypt. He desired to plant it and to establish it in the Promised Land. His nation was to act as a light to the other nations upon the earth, in order to draw the other nations of the earth to God.

However, the problem was that no one was able to keep all of the Law. Rather than humbly submitting to God and seeking God, which God would have graciously accepted, the people either openly rebelled against the Law (and therefore God) entirely and became just like the nations around them, or the Law (including the sacrifices for sin) became nothing but ritualism and legalism to them (i.e. the people acted out their part like hypocrites).

On the whole, therefore, the people did not genuinely seek after God, in faith, especially whenever they did not have good spiritual leaders to look up to, such as Moses, Joshua, Samuel, King David, King Hezekiah, or King Josiah (there are, of course, other examples of good spiritual leaders in scripture). Rather, the heart of the people grew hard and they kept God at a distance:-

> "Forasmuch as this people draw near me with their mouth, and with their lips do honour me, but have removed their heart far from me, and their fear toward me is taught by the precept of men." (KJV Isaiah 29:13)

There was nothing wrong with the Old Covenant. The Apostle Paul declared that, "the law is holy, and the commandment holy, and just, and good" (KJV Romans

48

7:12) and that, "the law is spiritual" (KJV Romans 7:14). The problem was that man was carnal and fleshly and in bondage to the law of sin and death. Man's heart was fundamentally evil and had a natural tendency to turn away from God.

Fallen man could not fulfil the law in his own natural strength, therefore, and the Law was clear as to what that led to:-

> "Cursed be he that confirmeth not all the words of this law to do them." (KJV Deuteronomy 27:26)

The Law, therefore, placed sinful man under a curse.

The Law had not only been given to show man what sin was (i.e. that which God declared to be sinful). The Law was also given to show man what *he* actually was (i.e. a sinner).

Moreover, the Law was also a revelation of God's own character. When you consider the Ten Commandments (Exodus 20:1-17), especially in light of the Sermon on the Mount (Matthew 5-7), you quickly realise that it was impossible for fallen man to fulfil the Law because the fulfilment of the Law required the living out of God's own life.

The Apostle Paul certainly found this to be true.

When we read Romans 7:15-24, we read of a man (i.e. the Apostle Paul) who tried all of his life to live out and perform all of the Law in his own natural strength. This is underlined by the fact that he referred to "I" so very often in these verses. "I" tried to do this. "I" tried to do that. However, "I" could not do this and

49

"I" could not do that. Paul realised that he could delight in the Law in his heart, but he did not have the power to fulfil the Law because the law of sin and death was at work within him. He rightly declared himself, therefore, to be a, "wretched man," as we all are.

However, that was not the end of the matter for Paul and, thankfully, it is not the end of the matter for us either. Long ago, God promised to do an entirely new thing for man:-

> "I will take you from among the heathen, and gather you out of all countries, and will bring you into your own land. Then will I sprinkle clean water upon you, and ye shall be clean: from all your filthiness, and from all your idols, will I cleanse you. A new heart also will I give you, and a new spirit will I put within you: and I will take away the stony heart out of your flesh, and I will give you a heart of flesh. And I will put my Spirit within you, and cause you to walk in My statutes, and ye shall keep My judgments, and do them. And ye shall be my people, and I will be your God." (KJV Ezekiel 36:24-28)

We saw that there is something fundamentally wrong with the heart of man in Chapters 4-6, since The Fall. We also saw how man is enslaved by the law of sin and death and it is this law that rules within the heart of fallen man. In order to put this right in man, God had to do a supernatural work in man. Man had to be delivered out of Satan's kingdom of darkness and brought into the kingdom of God. Man had to be cleansed. The personal spirit within a man had to be made new within him. Man also needed a new heart. Man then needed nothing short of the very life of God to be manifested within him, in order to cause man to follow God and to love and to worship God.

The Law could not do this.

The Law could show man what was good and what was evil. However, the Law did not have the power to change the heart of a man within him. Rather, the old man had to be put to death so that a new man could be formed and made. We see a graphic picture of this in Ezekiel 37 with the valley of dry bones.

Essentially, the valley of dry bones is a picture of the entire fallen race of man, from Adam to the last man that is yet to be born. They are all subject to the law of sin and death. They are all born spiritually dead and, thereafter, they all know physical death and decay. Everything that they inherited from Adam died and withered away. However, God was able to form, or raise up, or resurrect, an entirely new people from among the dry bones. God re-clothed them. God caused breath to enter into them. God opened up the graves, brought the people into a new kingdom and put his own Spirit within them so that they knew life.

God promised to do an entirely new thing:-

"Remember ye not the former things, neither consider the things of old. Behold, I will do a new thing; now it shall spring forth; shall ye not know it? I will even make a way in the wilderness, and rivers in the desert. The beast of the field shall honour Me, the dragons and the owls: because I give waters in the wilderness, and rivers in the desert, to give drink to My people, My chosen. This people have I formed for Myself; they shall show forth My praise." (KJV Isaiah 43:18-21)

The Law was holy and the Law was spiritual. However, sinful man was fleshly and carnal. Sinful man could not, therefore, perform, or fulfil, the Law. The problem was not with God, or His Law, or The Old Covenant. The problem was with sinful man and something radical had to be done.

Half measures were not sufficient.

The former things (i.e. the Old Covenant) had to be done away with so that new things (i.e. the New Covenant) could be ushered in:-

"No man putteth a piece of new cloth unto an old garment, for that which is put in to fill it up taketh from the garment, and the rent is made worse. Neither do men put new wine into old bottles: else the bottles break (or burst), and the wine runneth out, and the bottles perish: but they put new wine into new bottles, and both are preserved." (KJV Matthew 9:16-17)

What then do we see?

The Law and the Old Covenant did not bring life and God's Spirit cannot dwell in fallen man's old stony heart. An amendment of the Old Covenant, therefore, was not enough. It was also not sufficient to simply patch up the old heart within fallen man, as it was full of sin and was entirely unfit for purpose. The Old Covenant had to give way entirely to a New Covenant and man had to be given an entirely new heart in which God's own Spirit could dwell, but how could this be done?

God would send His only begotten Son to the earth to accomplish it.

Chapter 8

The Coming Of Christ

"The Holy Ghost shall come upon thee, and the power of the Highest shall overshadow thee; therefore also that holy thing which shall be born of thee shall be called the Son of God."
(KJV Luke 1:34)

"For the law was given by Moses, but grace and truth came by Jesus Christ."
(KJV John 1:17)

In Chapter 1, we saw that when the earth was made and was yet without form, or life, the Spirit of God was moving upon the face of the waters. The Holy Spirit foreshadowed, or overshadowed, the bringing forth of life upon the earth. When the angel, Gabriel, explained to Mary that she was going to conceive in her womb and bring forth a son and call His name Jesus (i.e. 'Jehovah the Saviour', or 'the Salvation of Jehovah'), Mary asked how that could happen. The method was strikingly similar to the creation account:-

> "The Holy Ghost shall come upon thee, and the power of the Highest shall overshadow thee: therefore also that holy thing which shall be born of thee shall be called the Son of God." (KJV Luke 1:34)

Jesus Christ was conceived through the holy seed of God and his conception was the beginning of the fulfilment of that which had been promised by God in Genesis 3:14-15. We begin to see then that Jesus was not of the seed, or progeny, of fallen Adam. Rather, Jesus was of the seed of God and an entirely new race began with the birth of Jesus.

In fact, Jesus is only the second true man to have ever walked upon the face of the earth after Adam (i.e. Adam, prior to Adam's fall). This is why Jesus is sometimes referred to as the second man.

The coming of Jesus Christ, the Messiah, had, of course, been foretold:-

> "And there shall come forth a Rod out of the stem of Jesse (who was King David's father), And a Branch shall grow out of his roots: and the Spirit of the LORD (i.e. 'Jehovah') shall rest upon Him, and the Spirit of wisdom and understanding, the Spirit of counsel and might, The Spirit of knowledge and of the fear of the LORD; and shall make Him of quick understanding in the fear of the LORD."
> (KJV Isaiah 11:1-4)

The Apostle John eloquently explained that, "the Word (i.e. the Word of God) was made flesh, and dwelt among us, (and we beheld His glory, the glory as of the only begotten of the Father), full of grace and truth" (KJV John 1:14). God, who is Spirit, became flesh and was born as a man (but a man without sin) upon the earth. "For in Him (i.e. in Jesus Christ) dwelleth all the fullness of the Godhead bodily" (KJV Colossians 2:9).

Jesus was, therefore, fully man and fully God. He was the brightness of His Father's glory and the express image of His Father's person (Hebrews 11:3).

Jesus, as a man upon the earth, was the exact expression of God the Father and the ultimate revelation of God to man.

Jesus was the very testimony of God upon the earth.

It ought not to surprise us, therefore, when Jesus said things such as, "he that hath seen Me hath seen the Father," (KJV John 14:9) and, "Believe Me that I am in the Father, and the Father in Me" (KJV John 14:11), "For it pleased the Father that in Him (i.e. in Jesus) should all fullness dwell" (KJV Colossians 1:19).

We also recall from Chapter 1 that God, who is Spirit and who is invisible, began to make Himself known in His creation. We see the culmination of that in the person of Jesus, whereby, "No man hath seen God at any time; the only-begotten Son, which is in the bosom of the Father, He hath declared Him" (KJV John 1:18). We also see that:-

> "[Jesus] is the image of the invisible God
> (i.e. not the image of fallen man, or of
> angels), the firstborn of every creature:
> for by Him were all things created that
> are in heaven, and that are in earth,
> visible and invisible, whether they be
> thrones, or dominions, or principalities,
> or powers, all things were created by
> Him, and for Him: and He is before all

things, and by Him all things consist."
(KJV Colossians 1:15-17)

All things had been created through the Word of God. The Word of God had become flesh and now the man, Jesus Christ, was, "upholding all things by the word of His power" (KJV Hebrews 1:3).

The great objective truth of reality (i.e. God) became flesh and He (i.e. Jesus) was rightfully able to declare, "I am the way, the truth, and the life" (KJV John 14:6).

Jesus Christ, the Son of God, was, and is, both fully man and fully God. However, Jesus set aside His deity and lived out His life upon the earth entirely as a man and not as God, in complete subjection to God His Father. This is why Jesus could truly say, "I say unto you, the Son can do nothing of Himself, but what He seeth the Father do; for what things soever He doeth (i.e. the Father), these also doeth the Son likewise" (KJV John 5:19).

Moreover, Jesus said, "I have not spoken of Myself; but the Father which sent Me, He gave me a commandment, what I should say, and what I should speak" (KJV John 12:49). Jesus came to do the will of His Father in heaven, therefore, and to finish the work that His Father had given Him to do and Jesus *delighted* in doing the will of His Father (John 4:34 and Psalm 40:8).

God is a faith being and we can see the relationship between God the Father, God the Word and God the Holy Spirit, which has been from everlasting to everlasting, being ratified upon the earth in God the Father, God the Son and God the Holy Spirit. The

Father made His will known to the Son (i.e. Jesus), the Son spoke out the word, in faith, and the Holy Spirit, being in perfect agreement with the Father and with the Son, caused the will of God to be done (i.e. the trinity acting as One in unity).

This was done in the person of Jesus Christ as a man upon the earth.

We also see, in the person of Jesus, the restoration of the perfect spiritual fellowship that God had with man in the Garden of Eden.

Jesus Christ was fully man and He lived out His life upon the earth as a man. Like any other man, Jesus had (and still has) His own personal spirit (i.e. the Spirit of Christ). However, the Spirit of Christ was not tainted by sin, or by The Fall. It was alive and in perfect subjection to, and in perfect loving fellowship with, God the Father.

Jesus spoke directly with His Father in heaven, as a man upon the earth, and the Father spoke directly with His Son, from heaven. The intuition of the Spirit of Christ was absolutely unhindered. God the Father could reveal all things to Jesus (i.e. into the Spirit of Christ), therefore, so that Jesus, as a man upon the earth, intuitively knew and understood the will of God.

Similarly, when Jesus was tempted, His conscience instantly recoiled, as the temptations were absolutely contrary to the will of His Father in heaven and He (i.e. Jesus) would not allow anything within Him to be at variance with the will of His Father in heaven. Jesus maintained perfect loving fellowship with His Father at all times.

As a man, Jesus also had (and still has) His own soul and His soul was in perfect subjection to His personal spirit and to His Father in heaven. By receiving perfect revelation from God, in His spirit, Jesus did not have to work out anything in His mind for Himself. He was simply able, in faith, to declare and to do the things that His Father told Him and showed Him.

Jesus also had (and still has) His own will and, as stated above, the disposition of His will was that He delighted to do the will of His Father in heaven (Psalm 40:8). Jesus Christ did not seek to do His own will, therefore, but only His Father's will.

Jesus also had (and still has) His own emotions and these were clearly seen at the death of His friend, Lazarus, (see John 11) and at the cleansing of the temple in Jerusalem (see Matthew 21, or the other Gospel accounts). However, the emotions of Jesus did not develop along the line of 'self'. His emotions were in complete subjection to His will. He did not get offended when He was personally attacked, therefore, as He had no pride in 'self'. However, when the Holy Spirit was blasphemed, or He found His Father's temple at Jerusalem being defiled, His zeal for God came to the fore.

Jesus had no 'self' life to defend.

Jesus also had a body as a man upon the earth. Although His body, or His features, were not anything to desire from an earthly point of view, His body was not a body of sin. Rather, it was the temple of the living God through whom the Father could live and move and have His Being.

What then can we say?

The man, Jesus Christ, grew up into perfection, as a man, and His soul developed up into all Godliness, as a man (Hebrews 2:10 and Hebrews 5:8-9).

Whereas Adam failed upon the earth, in the Garden of Eden, Jesus Christ did not fail as a man upon the earth (or, indeed, otherwise).

After Jesus was baptised (various baptisms are discussed in the Appendix) by John the Baptist in the river Jordan, He was led by the Holy Spirit into the wilderness where He was tempted and tested by Satan (Matthew 3-4). As with Adam and Eve, Satan tempted Jesus along the line of the lust of the eyes, the lust of the flesh and the pride of life.

Jesus had been in the wilderness, without food, for forty days, so being tempted to turn stones into bread would have been very tempting. This was akin to the fruit of the tree of the knowledge of good and evil, which was good to look at (i.e. the lust of the eyes) and was also good for food (i.e. the lust of the flesh).

Satan also tempted Jesus to throw Himself off the temple. This was also akin to the fruit of the tree of the knowledge of good and evil, as it was desired to make one wise (i.e. the pride of life). Jesus knew that He was the Son of God, and that He was loved by His Father, but He did not put His trust in His own personhood (i.e. the prideful disposition that His Father would save Him because of who He was).

Satan also offered Jesus all of the kingdoms of the earth. This was a real temptation when you recall that God had given the earth as a possession to Adam, but Adam had forfeited this, in the Garden of Eden, and surrendered possession of the earth to Satan. This was also akin to the fruit of the tree of the knowledge of good and evil, as the earth contained much to be looked at, was full of fleshly desires and it's ruler would be greatly revered (i.e. the lust of the eyes, the lust of the flesh and the pride of life).

Rather than considering each temptation, or arguing with Satan, Jesus simply rebuked Satan with scripture, at each turn, knowing that it was not the will of His Father in heaven to do anything that Satan was tempting Him to do.

Adam reasoned, did his own will and it brought death to all of mankind. Jesus, on the other hand, believed God and humbly obeyed that which His Father commanded, but what was it that His Father had ultimately commanded? Jesus told us, Himself, in John 12:49-50:-

> "For I have not spoken of Myself: but the Father which sent Me, He gave Me a commandment, what I should say, and what I should speak. And I know that His commandment is life everlasting: whatsoever I speak therefore, even as the Father said unto Me, so I speak." (KJV)

Adam's faithlessness to God in the Garden of Eden condemned man to slavery and death, but the faith of Jesus Christ opened up a new and living way into freedom and life everlasting.

So, what do we actually mean by the faith of Christ?

Chapter 9

The Faith Of Christ

"But now the righteousness of God without the law is manifested, being witnessed by the law and the prophets; even the righteousness of God which is by faith of Jesus Christ, unto all and upon them that believe."
(KJV Romans 3:21-22)

"For as by one man's disobedience many were made sinners, so by the obedience of one shall many be made righteous."
(KJV Romans 5: 19)

"For as in Adam all die, even so in Christ shall all be made alive."
(KJV 1 Corinthians 15:22)

"For God so loved the world, that He gave His only begotten Son, that whosoever believeth in Him should not perish, but have everlasting life. For God sent not His Son into the world to condemn the world; but that the world through Him might be saved."
(KJV John 3:16-17)

The many miracles, or signs, that God the Father did through Jesus, as a man upon the earth, are truly wonderful. They confirmed who Jesus actually was (i.e. the Son of God, the Christ, the Messiah). Jesus said

Himself, "Believe Me that I am in the Father, and the Father in Me: or else believe Me for the very works' sake" (KJV 14:11).

However, the many miracles, or signs, that were done through Jesus were, in a sense, only ancillary to what He had actually come to do. Jesus had come to do the will of His Father in heaven and the miracles, or signs, were a part of that. However, His Father had commanded, "life everlasting," (KJV John 12:50) and Jesus had to endure death on the cross in order for that commandment to be fulfilled.

It is staggering that Jesus described John the Baptist as, "more than a prophet," (KJV Matthew 11:9) and that, "Among them that are born of women there hath not risen a greater than John the Baptist" (KJV John 11:11). We read in Luke 1 that John the Baptist was filled with the Holy Spirit, even from his mother's womb, yes, but John the Baptist saw something in Jesus, the Messiah, that no one else had:-

> "Behold the Lamb of God, which taketh away the sins of the world." (KJV John 1: 29)

John the Baptist had understood that Jesus had come to the earth as the *Lamb* of God. He saw that Jesus was coming to be the great sacrifice to which all of the Law and the entire sacrificial system had pointed. Rather than simply covering sins, which is all that the Old Covenant could do, Jesus was coming to fulfil the Law, to take away the sins of the world and to reconcile all things to His Father in heaven, through His blood.

This could only be accomplished by Jesus on the cross.

We see then that Jesus, as a man, lived out a perfect life upon the earth, by faith. He lived out a life that was fully laid down and in complete subjection and obedience to His Father in heaven. Ultimately, such obedience to His Father culminated in Jesus laying down His life upon the cross (John 10:18). When Jesus died upon the cross, for the sins of the whole world, He became the perfect and final sacrifice that was required in order to reconcile all things to His Father in heaven.

By faith, Jesus trusted His Father and He obeyed His Father into death.

Jesus became sin upon the cross (2 Corinthians 5:21) and the very power, or principle, of sin was destroyed in Jesus when He died upon the cross. The law of sin and death was brought to nothing in Jesus. Death was put to death and the very power of Satan, and of darkness, was destroyed.

We see then the fulfilment, in Jesus, of what God had promised in Genesis 3:15 whereby Jesus, as a man, crushed the head of Satan upon the cross.

When Jesus died upon the cross, He, "descended first into the lower parts of the earth," (KJV Ephesians 4:9) and, "preached unto the spirits in prison," to those, "which sometime were disobedient, when once the longsuffering of God waited in the days of Noah" (KJV 1 Peter 3:19-21). We see here the great mercy of God, whereby the good news of salvation was pre-figured through Noah, the preacher of righteousness, so Jesus went to preach the gospel to those that preceded the preaching of Noah (i.e. to those who had died prior to, and as a result of, the flood, having never heard the gospel). In so doing, Jesus led captivity captive. He bound the strong man and freed the prisoners (Judges 5:12, Psalm 68:18 and Ephesians 4:8).

Prior to His death, Jesus explained that he had, "a baptism to be baptised with," (KJV Luke 12:49). This baptism was death upon the cross, burial and, thereafter, resurrection. Having preached the gospel to those in death and hades (i.e. hell), Jesus was:-

> "...declared (i.e. continually declared) to be the Son of God with power, according to the Spirit of holiness, by the resurrection from the dead." (KJV Romans 1:4)

People sometimes struggle with the idea that Jesus went down into death and hades (i.e. hell). However, Jesus became sin and, "the wages of sin is death" (KJV Romans 6:23). It was just and equitable, therefore, that Jesus went to hell. Moreover, hell was created by God and God is sovereign in all of His creation. We do well to remember that King David wrote the following:-

> "Whither shall I go from Thy Spirit? Or whither shall I flee from Thy presence? If I ascend up into heaven, Thou (i.e. God) art there: If I make my bed in hell (i.e. death and hades), behold, Thou art there." (KJV Psalm 139:7-8)

> "Thou will not leave My soul in hell (i.e. death and hades), Neither will Thou

suffer Thine Holy One to see corruption." (KJV Psalm 16:10)

What then can we say?

Jesus died for the sins of the entire world, He went down into hell, preached the gospel to the captives, was searched and tried by the Holy Spirit, Who could find no fault in Him, and, by raising Him (i.e. Jesus) from the dead, by the power of His right hand, God the Father declared Him (i.e. Jesus) to be the Son of God, with power, through the resurrection (i.e. the resurrection of Jesus from the dead was, in itself, the powerful declaration that Jesus was the Son of God). Having been raised by His Father, Jesus, "is gone into heaven, and is on the right hand of God; angels and authorities and powers being made subject unto Him" (KJV 1 Peter 3:22).

Let us remember that Jesus accomplished this all, as a man, by faith.

Jesus was a man, without sin, filled with the Holy Spirit, being One with His Father in heaven. By faith, Jesus obeyed His Father and willingly laid down His life upon the cross through the Holy Spirit (Hebrews 9:14). The blood of Jesus was shed on the cross. The Father looked upon the blood and was satisfied that the blood was sufficient for sin and for all sins (i.e. from Adam to the last person ever to be born). The Father had faith in the Son to accomplish the work and the Son had faith in the Father to raise Him from the dead.

We read in scripture that, "we believe on Him (i.e. the Father) that raised up Jesus our Lord from the dead; who was delivered for our offences, and was raised again for our justification" (KJV Romans 4:25).

Another translation of this verse is that Jesus, "was raised *because* of our justification," and the implication of this is staggering. If the Father had looked upon the blood of Jesus and judged that it was not sufficient for our justification (i.e. it could not atone for sin and all sins), then the Father would not have raised Jesus from among the dead. However, the Father did look upon the blood and did judge that it was sufficient for the atonement of sin and all sins.

Glory to God!

The Law had shown man that God was utterly holy and that man was utterly sinful, or, at least, it should have. Man could not fulfil all of the Law and, as such, man could not be declared just, or righteous. However, the second man, Jesus Christ, finished the work that His Father gave Him to do and He won salvation for man.

Salvation was won by the faith of Christ:-

"...knowing that a man is not justified by the works of the law, but by the faith of Jesus Christ, even we have believed in Jesus Christ, that we might be justified by the faith of Christ, and not the works of the law: for by the works of the law shall no flesh be justified." (KJV Galatians 2:16)

"...not having my own righteousness, which is of the law, but that which is through the faith of Christ, the righteousness which is of God by faith." (KJV Philippians 3:9)

It may surprise the reader, but the faith that was exercised by Jesus, as a man upon the earth, had never been seen upon the earth, in a man, before. A picture of this faith was seen in Abraham (i.e. the father of faith) whereby Abraham, "believed in the LORD (i.e. Jehovah) and he (i.e. Jehovah) counted it to him (i.e. Abraham) for righteousness" (KJV Genesis 15:6). Abraham believed God before the Law was given and God counted Abraham's faith as righteousness (i.e. the righteousness that is by faith, apart from the Law). Abraham received his promised son, Isaac, therefore, and his descendants became as numerous as the grains of sand on the sea shore. However, Jesus Christ faithfully fulfilled all of the Law and the prophets, by his own faith, so that we could all receive the promise of salvation and be declared righteous in Christ Jesus.

The Law had served its purpose, but now the faith of Christ had come:-

> "But the scripture hath concluded all under sin, that the promise by faith of Jesus Christ might be given to them that believe. But before faith came (i.e. the faith of Christ), we were kept under the law, shut up unto the faith which should afterwards be revealed (i.e. revealed in Christ)." (KJV Galatians 3:22-23)

Salvation was entirely won for us, therefore, by the *grace* of *God* and by the *faith* of *Jesus Christ*.

Did we have anything to do with the salvation that was won for us? No. Did we contribute, in any

68

way, to the salvation that was won for us? No. Did our own faith play any part? No. It absolutely did not and this is clearly stated in scripture:-

> "For by grace (i.e. the grace of God) are ye saved through faith (i.e. the faith of Christ); and that not of yourselves: it is the gift of God (i.e. salvation is the gift of God): not of works (i.e. the works of the Law), lest any man should boast. For we are His (i.e. God's) workmanship, created in Christ Jesus unto good works, which God hath before ordained that we should walk in them." (KJV Ephesians 2:8-9)

The works of the Law and all of the sacrifices that were made under the Old Covenant could not bring salvation to the world, therefore, but the grace of God and the faithful obedience of Jesus Christ could. How fitting it is, therefore, that scripture records, "to obey is better than sacrifice" (1 Samuel 15:22).

Everything that already pertains to salvation has already been accomplished by the grace of God and by the faith of Jesus Christ, who is the, "author and finisher (or perfecter) of faith" (KJV Hebrews 12:2).

Man, though fallen, was created in the image of God. God has given light to every man (KJV John 1:9), so that every man may believe. Every man must exercise his own faith, therefore, and choose to believe into Jesus Christ and the salvation that He has won for us.

However, what does man actually enter into if he does choose to believe?

Chapter 10

The Law Of The Spirit Of Life In Christ Jesus

"The thief cometh not, but for to steal and to kill, and to destroy: I am come that they might have life, and that they might have it more abundantly."
(KJV John 10:10)

"I am the resurrection, and the life: he that believeth in Me, though he were dead, yet shall he live: and whosoever liveth and believeth in Me shall never die."
(KJV John 11:25)

"And this is life eternal, that they might know Thee (i.e. the Father) the only true God, and Jesus Christ, whom Thou hast sent."
(KJV John 17:3)

"For the wages of sin is death; but the gift of God is eternal life through Jesus Christ our Lord."
(KJV Romans 6:23)

John the Baptist is recorded, in scripture, as saying, "He that believeth on the Son hath everlasting life," (KJV John 3:36) and Jesus, Himself, said that, "I am come that they might have life, and that they might have it more abundantly" (KJV John 10:10). The only

71

way for this to be accomplished was through the death, burial and resurrection of Jesus.

It should not surprise us, therefore, that if we wish to enter into this life, we likewise must know death, burial and resurrection. That was certainly the reality for the Apostle Paul:-

> "I am crucified with Christ: nevertheless I live; yet not I, but Christ liveth in me; and the life which I now live in the flesh (i.e. in the body) I live by the faith of the Son of God, who loved me, and gave Himself for me." (KJV Galatians 2:20)

> "God forbid that I should glory, save in the cross of our Lord Jesus Christ, by whom the world is crucified unto me, and I unto the world." (KJV Galatians 6:14)

Jesus had lived out a perfect life upon the earth, as a man, and He obediently laid down His life on the cross for sin and for the sins of the whole world. Thereafter, He was buried and God the Father raised Him from among the dead. Jesus Christ is now seated, as a man, in heaven, at the right hand of God the Father.

Death, burial and resurrection are at the heart of salvation and the Apostle Paul was emphatic on this crucial point:-

> "Know ye not, that so many of us as were baptised into Jesus were baptised into His death? Therefore we are buried with Him by baptism into death: that like as

Christ was raised up from the dead by the glory of the Father, even so we also should walk in newness of life. For if we have been planted together in the likeness of His death, we shall be also ...of...resurrection." (KJV Romans 6:3-5)

We see then that baptism truly means death, burial and resurrection. If we have believed into the Son of God, we have gone down into death with Him, we have been buried with Him and His own resurrected life has been raised up in us.

We recall the picture of the valley of the dry bones in Ezekiel 37 and realise that we, who are of Adam's fallen race, have gone down into death and have been buried, so that we may be raised up a new creation. We are raised up an entirely new race in Christ Jesus, which is totally separate from the race of Adam. This is why Jesus is sometimes referred to as the last Adam (i.e. the second man and the last Adam). The old race of Adam is cut off in Christ Jesus and an entirely new race is created:-

"Knowing this, that our old man (i.e. the sinful nature that we inherited from Adam) is crucified with [Jesus], that the body of sin might be destroyed, that henceforth we should not serve sin. For he that is dead (i.e. us) is freed from sin. Now if we be dead with Christ, we believe that we shall also live with Him: knowing that Christ being raised from the dead dieth no more; death hath no more dominion over Him. For in that He died, He died unto sin once, but in that He liveth, He liveth unto God. Likewise reckon ye also yourselves to be dead indeed unto sin, but alive unto God through Jesus Christ our Lord." (KJV Romans 6:6-11)

We have been crucified with Christ. We have died. Our old sinful nature has gone down into death and it has been buried. We are no longer slaves to the law of sin and death.

Similarly, the Law (i.e. as given to Moses) no longer applies to us because we have died. We, "are become dead to the law by the body of Christ," (KJV Romans 7:4) so that we may be married to Christ (Romans 7).

Jesus said, "Think not that I am come to destroy the law, or the prophets: I am not come to destroy, but to fulfil" (KJV Matthew 5:17). Jesus Christ has fulfilled the Law and the prophets and He has blotted, "out the handwriting of ordinances that was against us (i.e. the Law), which was contrary to us, and took it out of the way, nailing it to His cross" (KJV Colossians 2:14). We have died to the Law and the Law has died to us, being nailed to the cross.

We are freed, therefore, from the Law and freed from the law of sin and death:-

"Let not sin therefore reign in your mortal body, that ye should obey it in the lusts thereof. Neither yield ye your members as instruments of unrighteousness unto sin: but yield (i.e. humble) yourselves unto God, as those that are alive from the dead, and your members as instruments of righteousness unto God. For sin shall not have dominion over you: for ye are not under the law, but under grace." (KJV Romans 6:12-14)

"...they that are Christ's have crucified the flesh with the affections and lusts." (KJV Galatians 5:24)

What then are we saying?

We are saying that our sins are forgiven by the blood of Christ. However, we are also saying that the very power, or principle, of sin was destroyed by Jesus upon the cross. We are no longer slaves to the law of sin and death and we are no longer subject to the Law that was against us, as it has been fulfilled by Jesus and nailed to His cross.

Salvation in the New Covenant, therefore, is not simply the forgiveness of sins. The very power, or principle, of sin has been absolutely broken in us because it was absolutely broken in Christ and Christ dwells in our hearts by faith (Ephesians 3:17).

Some may then say, well what about Romans 7:14-24?

Paul described himself as a, "wretched man," because of the predicament in which he had found himself to be. Elsewhere, Paul described himself as the chief sinner (1 Timothy 1:15). Paul's experience was that "I" tried to do this and "I" tried to do that, but he found that "he" could not do this and that "he" could not do that.

Surely if Paul did not know freedom from sin, then how can we expect to?

The point that Paul was making in these passages was that "he", who was from Adam, could not fulfil the Law *in his own natural strength*. "He" simply could not do it because another law was at work in his members, which was the law of sin and death. However, Paul then knew what it was to be crucified with Christ (Galatians 2:20). The "I" in Paul tried to do this and tried to do that *in his own natural strength*, but Paul then knew that the "I" in Paul had been crucified.

Paul had been out to death.

Paul also knew that if the law of sin and death was to work in him again (i.e. if he gave into the old 'self' life) he really would be the vilest of sinners (i.e. raising up again the old life that had been crucified). Apart from the grace of God, that is what we all are by nature: the vilest of sinners.

However, Paul did not end the matter by woefully crying out in despair, "who shall deliver me from the body of this death!" (KJV Romans 7:24). Instead, Paul explained who actually *had* delivered him from the body of this death by declaring, "I thank God through Jesus Christ our Lord" (KJV Romans 7:25).

Paul was not acknowledging defeat, or describing a partial, or faulty, salvation. He was declaring complete victory in Jesus Christ:-

> "There is therefore now no condemnation to them which are in Christ Jesus, who walk not after the flesh, but after the

Spirit. For the law of the Spirit of life in Christ Jesus [hath] made me free from the law of sin and death. For what the law could not do, in that it was weak through flesh, God sending His own Son in the likeness of sinful flesh, and for sin, condemned sin in the flesh: that the righteousness of the law might be fulfilled in us, who walk not after the flesh, but after the Spirit." (KJV Romans 8:1-4)

"Therefore, brethren, we are debtors, not to the flesh to live after the flesh. For if ye live after the flesh, ye shall die: but if ye through the Spirit (i.e. by the grace of God) do mortify the deeds of the body ye shall live. For as many as are led by the Spirit of God, they are the sons of God." (KJV Romans 8:12-14)

We see then that we have been put to death and that the law of sin and death has, itself, been put to death within us. A new law is now at work within us that works by meekness, lowliness and humility; the law of the Spirit of life that is in Christ Jesus.

Glory to God!

Being of the fallen race of Adam and being subject to the law of sin and death, we were unable to fulfil the Law and we truly were a wretched race, as Paul saw. However, Christ died for us and, when He died, He destroyed the law of sin and death in His flesh and He fulfilled the Law and the prophets. He can now fulfil

77

this in every single person who comes to Him in faith and who faithfully abides in Him, as He is the resurrection and the life that His Father had commanded.

How then is this accomplished in us?

God has ever pleaded with man to return to Him in humility (Micah 6:8), but He does not force man to return to Him. "Yea, I (i.e. God) have loved thee (i.e. man) with an everlasting love: Therefore with lovingkindness have I drawn thee," (KJV Jeremiah 31:3). "And ye (i.e. man) shall seek me and find Me (i.e. God), when ye shall search for Me with all your heart" (KJV Jeremiah 29:13). "Without faith it is impossible to please Him (i.e. God): for he (i.e. man) that cometh to God must believe that He is, and that He is a rewarder of them that diligently seek Him" (KJV Hebrews 11:6).

Jesus also said, "seek thee first the kingdom of God, and His righteousness" (KJV Matthew 6:33).

What then are we saying?

God has cried out to man, but man must answer the call and cry out to God.

Part of the work of the Holy Spirit is to convict the heart of man of sin. We will recall how the Spirit of God was moving upon the face of the waters when the earth was created, but was yet without life. The Spirit of God also moves upon the heart of man to convict, or convince, him of his sins, so that man may turn (i.e. repent) from his evil ways and seek God for His Salvation (i.e. Jesus Christ).

Jesus came to fulfil the Law and the prophets, not to destroy them. This is why He could say, "Till heaven and earth pass, one jot or one tittle shall in no wise pass from the law, till all be fulfilled" (KJV Matthew 5:18). The Law remains, but it only now applies to those who are not continually abiding in Jesus Christ because, "if ye be led of the Spirit, ye are not under the law" (KJV Galatians 5:18). The Law remains to show the character of God to sinful man, therefore, as well as the utter sinfulness of sin and the utter sinfulness of the heart of man. It is upon these things that the Holy Spirit is able to convict sinful man of his sin.

Jesus Christ is the Saviour of the whole world and salvation has already been won for us by the grace of God and by the faith of Jesus Christ. All that is left for man to do is to decide to give his entire life to Jesus, by faith. Once man does that, he is declared just in the sight of God. His sins are forgiven by the blood of Christ and he can, thereafter, enter into the full salvation of God.

However, what do we mean when we say that we are saved?

The forgiveness of sins is glorious and God will graciously forgive us our sins. However, the forgiveness of sins, alone, does not cause us to enter into the fullness of salvation. The forgiveness of sins does not change our nature. So, what does it truly mean to be saved? What are we actually saved from?

When we wholly give ourselves to Jesus Christ, by faith, we become crucified with Christ. The old sinful nature within us, which is subject to the law of sin and death, dies. All that we inherited from Adam is put to death and it is buried. The Holy Spirit overshadows us and fills us and births the very life of Jesus Christ into our hearts. We are born again, "not of blood, nor of the will of the flesh, nor of the will of man, but of God" (KJV John 1:13). We are, "strengthened with might by His Spirit in the inner man (i.e. in our hearts): that Christ

79

may dwell in [our] hearts by faith" (KJV Ephesians 3:16-17) and God our Father is also in us all (Ephesians 4:6).

God is not simply gracious to us in the New Covenant, as He was gracious to people in the Old Covenant under the Law. "For the law was given by Moses, but grace and truth came by Jesus Christ" (KJV John 1:17). The grace of God is birthed within us in the New Covenant, therefore, so that the very life of God is at work within us, willing and doing of His own good pleasure (Philippians 2:13). We are, "kept by the power of God," (KJV 1 Peter 1:5) so that God causes us to walk in His ways (Ezekiel 36:27).

We see then that we are filled with the Holy Spirit and God the Father and the God the Son both dwell in our hearts. It may surprise the reader, but we actually enter into a much better position than that which Adam ever attained in the Garden of Eden!

Let us look at it another way.

Jesus, as a man upon the earth, was filled with the Holy Spirit and was one with His Father in heaven. It pleased all the fullness of God to dwell in Him (Colossians 1:19). Jesus even said that if anyone saw Him that they had seen the Father (John 14:9). Jesus Christ was, therefore, the testimony of God upon the earth (i.e. God in Christ). When we enter into salvation, we see one further step, which is God, in Christ, in us.

When God looks at us, individually, and when God looks at the Church (i.e. at Saints corporately), He sees Jesus Christ straight away, even if we are still only babes (or little children) in Christ. However, as we grow up from being babes (or little children) in Christ and grow up into being young men and, perhaps thereafter, into fathers (1 John 2:12-14), people in the world around us (and even the angels and the powers and principalities) should ultimately see Christ.

We are, therefore, the testimony of Jesus Christ upon the earth.

In the Old Covenant, God was continually covering the sins of the people because the Law and the sacrificial system could not change the heart of a man within him. In the New Covenant, "If we confess our sins, He (i.e. God) is faithful and just to forgive us our sins, and to cleanse us from all unrighteousness" (KJV 1 John 1:9). We can confess our sins day and daily, therefore, and God will graciously forgive us (which is not, of course, a licence for us to sin). Our sins are not simply covered in the New Covenant; they are entirely done away with.

Moreover, in the New Covenant, when we go down into death and burial and become of resurrection, God also renews a right spirit within us and He gives us an entirely new heart (the fulfilment of Ezekiel 36:24-27). Spiritual fellowship between man and God is restored. The Holy Spirit fills our heart, Jesus Christ and God the Father dwell in our heart and God's own life, in Christ Jesus, is lived out in us so that we are declared righteous and so that righteousness is actually maintained in us. The very life that Jesus lived as a man upon the earth is lived out in us.

The New Covenant is much more glorious, therefore, than the Old Covenant.

The grace of God is at work in us (i.e. God's own life is at work in us). The love of God is within us (i.e. God's own love, or 'agape' love). The faith of Christ is in us (i.e. the faith that can move mountains, even if it is only a mustard seed size). The obedience and faithfulness of Christ is in us (i.e. the obedience and faithfulness by which Jesus laid His own life down). The righteousness of Christ is in us (i.e. the very righteousness of God).

The power of sin is broken in Christ and, as we abide in Christ, the very power of sin is broken in us too. Satan has no power over us because he has absolutely no power over Christ. God does not give us salvation, therefore, as a commodity.

God gives Himself to us.

What then is the natural outworking of God's own life within us?

As Jesus lives out His life in us, He also fulfils the Law within us because He has already fulfilled the Law and the prophets and, in that sense, we remain under law to Christ (1 Corinthians 9:21). Commandments found in the Old Testament, therefore, become the natural outworking of Christ abiding in our hearts.

For example, "Thou shalt love the LORD thy God (i.e. 'Jehovah', 'Elohim') with all thine heart, and with all thy soul, and with all thy might," (KJV Deuteronomy 6:4) and, "Thou shalt love thy neighbour as thyself" (KJV Leviticus 19:18) and, "Thou shalt not kill," (KJV Leviticus 19:13) and, "Thou shall not commit adultery," (KJV Leviticus 19:14) etc. were all impossible for fallen man to fully obey, especially when viewed in light of the Sermon on the Mount that Jesus preached (Matthew 5-7). However, Christ now dwells in our hearts, by faith, and we are filled with the love of God. The natural outworking of Christ's life in us is that we will, in fact, love the LORD our God with all our

82

hearts, we will love our neighbours as ourselves, we won't kill and we won't commit adultery; not even in our hearts.

Glory to God!

The Law is no longer written upon stone tablets (Jeremiah 31:31-33). Rather, God's own nature, in Christ Jesus, is written upon the fleshly tables of our heart by the Holy Spirit (2 Corinthians 3:3). The Law and the Sermon on the Mount become the natural disposition and outworking of our heart, therefore, because God's own nature, in Christ, dwells in our hearts.

Living as a saint then (i.e. the normal Christian life) becomes natural to us.

It is no wonder that the Apostle John wrote, "My little children, these things I write unto you, that ye sin not" (KJV 1 John 2:1). It was not John's expectation that we should sin, for we have been set free from sin.

Of course, John acknowledged that we all have sinned (1 John 1:10), but sin is no longer the natural disposition of our hearts. We may unconsciously sin and the blood of Christ is continually sprinkled on our behalf for such sins (Hebrews 12:24), but conscious sin is no longer our natural disposition. To sin consciously now is to act wilfully against the law of the Spirit of life in Christ Jesus that is now at work in us (i.e. to sin wilfully now is to resurrect our old sinful 'self' nature and to act against the new nature that is within us, so that we once again become slaves to the law of sin and death).

As Paul would say, "God forbid!" (KJV Romans 6:15).

Having been crucified with Christ, each of us must take up our own cross, daily, and die to self, daily, to ensure that nothing of our old nature resurfaces. We find then that 'self' is the great enemy and that we must, "through the Spirit (i.e. through the grace of God)…mortify the deeds of the body" (KJV Romans 8:13). We must not give even an inch to the flesh, for it is contrary to the Spirit and we cannot serve two masters (Matthew 6:24).

We must also be, "renewed in the spirit of [our minds]," (KJV Ephesians 4:23) for we retain our old memories (and thought patterns) and Satan will continue to tempt us along the line of our flesh and along the line of our old thoughts and minds. However, "God is faithful, who will not suffer you to be tempted above that ye are able, but will with the temptation also make a way to escape, that ye may be able to bear it" (KJV 1 Corinthians 10:13).

We also do well to remember that, "greater is He (i.e. God) that is in [us], than he (i.e. Satan) that is in the world" (KJV 1 John 4:4). We are not to reason with Satan, or the world. Rather, we must believe God and humbly submit to God, so that the grace of God within us overcomes Satan and the world, remembering that, "we wrestle not against flesh and blood, but against principalities, against powers, against the rulers of the darkness of this world, against spiritual wickedness in high places" (KJV Ephesians 6:12).

Only Christ within us can overcome these things (Ephesians 6:13-18).

"We [also] have the mind of Christ," (KJV 1 Corinthians 2:16) and we must, faithfully, believe what God has said in respect of salvation. We must, therefore, fully enter into the fullness of the salvation that has been won for us. Otherwise, we will not believe, or we will believe along a lesser line, and will be as the children of Israel who, "could not enter in[to the promised land] because of unbelief" (KJV Hebrews 3:19).

It is no wonder, therefore, that scripture declares, "If ye will not believe, surely ye shall not be established" (KJV Isaiah 7:9).

What then are we saying?

We have been purchased at a great price and we are no longer our own (1 Corinthians 6:20). Even as Christ laid down His life, so we must lay down our lives by the power of the Holy Spirit. Jesus said, "He that findeth his life shall lose it: and he that loseth his life for My sake shall find it" (KJV Matthew 10:39). We must lay our lives down upon the altar as living sacrifices before God, therefore, so that all that pertains to the old man is burnt up and consumed (i.e. the end of the flesh), so that the beauty of Christ may be raised up in us (Isaiah 61:3).

Our, "life is hid with Christ in God" (KJV Colossians 3:3).

Christ is our life. We must, therefore, become less and He must become all in all within us. "Death worketh in us," (KJV 2 Corinthians 4:12) so that this life may work in us and, thereafter, in others. If we do not have such a spirit within us (i.e. the Spirit of Christ that lays down its life before God in meekness, lowliness and humility), then we are not of God and cannot expect to receive the promise of God (Romans 8:9). "How shall we escape if we neglect so great salvation[?]" (KJV Hebrews 2:3). Rather, we must fully believe in the fullness of the salvation that God has won for us, so that we may fully enter into the fullness of the salvation that

God has won for us. We must believe what God has said is true.

So, what is the sum?

We are given new hearts. A right spirit is renewed within us. Christ sits upon the throne of our hearts and we have wholeheartedly laid down our lives before Him; spirit, soul and body. We are filled with the Holy Spirit and God the Father and God the Son both dwell in our hearts. Spiritual fellowship with God has been restored. The Spirit of Truth has come and He is guiding us into all truth (John 16). As we receive from God and walk in the light that He has given us (i.e. as we obey Him and abide in Him), our very souls develop along the line of Godliness, as God had always intended for mankind, and our bodies truly do become the temples of the living God. As we faithfully abide in Christ, the fruits of the Holy Spirit are manifested within us (i.e. the love, joy, peace, longsuffering, gentleness, goodness, faith, meekness and temperance mentioned in Galatians 5:22) and we are known by the fruits of the Spirit. We truly then do become the salt of the earth, as a sweet savour of Christ, and we also become a lampstand upon the earth to display the glory of God.

How is this glory seen?

When Jesus died upon the cross He, "spoiled principalities and powers, He made a shew of them openly, triumphing over them in it" (KJV Colossians 2:15). Jesus did this as a man:-

> "to the intent that now unto the principalities and powers in heavenly places might be known by the church the manifold wisdom of God, according to

the eternal purpose which He purposed in Christ Jesus our Lord." (KJV Ephesians 3:10-11)

The glory of God can now be seen in Christ, in His Church, by every man, woman and child upon the earth and also by the angels and by Satan and by all of the fallen angels.

The invisible God is now being seen and glorified in man, who was created for the glory of God (Isaiah 43:7) and to show forth His praise (Isaiah 43:21).

The New Covenant is much greater than the Old Covenant. We must not, therefore, get stuck striving in the Old Covenant.

We also recall that Jesus said, "Among them that are born of women there hath not risen a greater than John the Baptist" (KJV Matthew 11:11), who lived in the Old Covenant. However, "he that is least in the kingdom of heaven (i.e. in the New Covenant) is greater than he (i.e. John the Baptist)." Why, on this side of eternity, are we considered greater than John the Baptist and greater than Enoch, Noah, Abraham, Isaac, Jacob, Joseph, Moses, Joshua, Samuel, Kind David, King Hezekiah, King Josiah, Elijah, Elisha and many others? It is because we have God's own life, in Christ, abiding in us.

Let us look at an example from scripture:-

"Consider the lilies of the field, how they grow: they toil not, neither do they spin: and yet I say unto you, That even Solomon in all his glory was not arrayed like one of these." (KJV Matthew 6:28-29)

Solomon was born of the fallen race of Adam. The natural outworking of his heart was the law of sin and death and that was how his heart developed. God graciously clothed Solomon, externally, with finery and riches, but that could not change Solomon's heart within him. The Old Covenant only covered up the old man externally. However, salvation has now been won for us by the grace of God and by the faith of Jesus Christ. God has given us a new heart and has clothed us, internally, with Christ.

Lilies naturally grow up into something beautiful. As Christ abides in our hearts by faith, and as we obey Him and walk in the light that He has given us, we cannot help but grow up into anything other than the beauty of our Lord Jesus Christ. We, therefore, become holy and something entirely 'other than' the world and the people of the world.

Moreover, the very words that our Lord Jesus Christ speaks are not of the world. Rather, they are "spirit," and, "life," (KJV John 6:63) and, as He speaks through us, our words become spirit and life to those around us so that we, thereby, wash one another's feet and cleanse one another.

We are not, merely, simply patched up versions of our old selves.

In the New Covenant, the Holy Spirit does not simply come alongside us in order to help us to imitate Jesus Christ. The Christ life *cannot* be *imitated* by us. Rather, the Holy Spirit indwells us so that the life of God in Christ is birthed within us. As we abide in that life we bear fruit and become worshipers of God in spirit and in truth (John 4:23), but we find that, apart from that life, we can do absolutely nothing in the kingdom of God (John 15:5).

Similarly, the Holy Spirit does not fill us so that we are empowered to get on with 'doing our own things' for God and, thereafter, seek His blessing in those things. The Holy Spirit comes so that we are brought to the end of our 'selves' (i.e. our own thoughts, hopes and ambitions) so that God may live out His own life in us and will and do of His own good pleasure in us. We are not to live out our own lives, therefore, in the strength of the Holy Spirit and, thereafter, ask God to bless it. Rather, God has clothed Himself with us so that He may live out His own life in us.

The life that Jesus lived upon the earth, as a man, is the normal Christian life and that life can now be lived out in us. We are not perfect, but the life of Christ within us is absolutely perfect. As we learn to die to self, the life of Christ within us becomes all in all so that we are continually perfected in Christ Jesus.

God did not win a faulty, or incomplete, salvation for us. However, we will not enter into the fullness of the salvation that has been won for us if we insist upon living out our own lives.

God forbid!

God said to Moses at the commencement of the Old Covenant, "Thou canst not see my face: for there shall no man see me, and live" (KJV Exodus 33:20). The same is true for us in the New Covenant. When we meet with the living God, our 'self' life dies in His presence and, when we see Jesus face to face, in glory, we will know the absolute fullness of this truth.

Accordingly, we must lay down our lives and deliberately fellowship with God so that Christ becomes in us, "a well of water springing up into everlasting life" (KJV John 4:14). "For as the Father hath life in Himself; so hath He given to the Son to have life in Himself," (KJV John 5:26) to the end that we may, "know the love of Christ, which passeth knowledge, that [we] might be filled with all the fullness of God" (KJV Ephesians 3:19).

For we, "are built up a spiritual house, a holy priesthood," (KJV 1 Peter 2:5) and, "a kingdom of priests," (KJV Exodus 19:6) with Jesus Christ as our great high priest (Hebrews 4:14).

Like the levitical priesthood that preceded us, our inheritance is not in fleshly, or earthly, things. Rather, God is our inheritance (Numbers 18:20), our shield, our exceedingly great reward (Genesis 15:1) and our portion forever (Psalm 73:26) and we are also God's own inheritance (Ephesians 1:18).

We begin to see then how blessed it is to, "be in subjection to the Father of spirits, and live" (KJV Hebrews 12:9).

We are one with Christ and we have entered into the perfect fellowship of love that God the Father, God the Word and God the Holy Spirit have known from everlasting to everlasting. This is what we have entered into, down here, as saints upon the earth.

"As He is (i.e. Christ), so are we in this world" (KJV 1 John 4:17). We may, therefore, "all come in the unity of the faith (i.e. the faith of Christ), and unto the knowledge of the Son of God, unto a perfect man, [and] unto the measure of the stature of the fullness of Christ," (KJV Ephesians 4:13) as saints upon the earth.

God has, "blessed us with all spiritual blessings in heavenly places in Christ" (KJV Ephesians 1:3). We start to know this tremendous truth (and the joy of it) upon the earth and we will know the fullness of it all on the other side of eternity when we see Jesus face to face in our new resurrection bodies.

This is what Jesus died for. This is what Jesus was raised for. This is what Jesus has won for us.

This is New Covenant Salvation.

Appendix

'Baptism'

Talking about baptism can be a risky endeavour. Almost every Christian denomination upon the face of the earth has its own exact doctrine, or interpretation, as to what baptism really is. It is even prevalent among man that we can all understand something the same way, basically, yet explain it in quite different terms from one another. Unfortunately, this can sometimes lead to sharp disagreements and even splits in Churches. This is partly why there are so many different Christian denominations.

When talking about baptism, therefore, we have to be careful to identify what baptism we actually mean. Let us look at some of the baptisms (plural) referred to in the scriptures.

Noah was described as, "a preacher of righteousness," in 2 Peter 2:5 (KJV). Noah believed God and built the ark, "wherein few, that is, eight souls were saved by water" (KJV 1 Peter 3:20). This was an example of the righteousness that is by faith, apart from the Law, but it was also an early picture of baptism. God judged the sins of the world in the days of Noah and He sent a flood to destroy all the flesh of mankind, save those eight people that were in the ark, as "the wickedness of man was great in the earth, and…the imagination of the thoughts of his heart was only evil continually" (KJV Genesis 6:5). Sin was judged and we see the general principle of baptism at work in the death and burial of the old world and the birth of a new world. Noah and his family literally could not go back to the old world because it had been destroyed by the flood, but they could make a new start in the new world after the flood. Noah and his family were graciously saved by God. However, the heart of man was not changed.

Even in Noah's day, we see the principle of death, burial and resurrection.

Moses leading the children of Israel out of the bondage of Egypt is a clearer picture of baptism. The children of Israel had been in the bondage of Egypt for upwards of four hundred years. Egypt, at that time, was the most powerful nation on earth and it was filled with all sorts of idolatry and beliefs that were completely contrary to God. Whereas Moses believed God and instructed the children of Israel to place the blood of lambs on the lintel and side posts of their doors, so that the judgment of God would pass over them, the Egyptians did not believe God and God, "smote all the firstborn in the land of Egypt" (KJV Exodus 12:29). Thereafter, the Egyptians thrust the children of Israel out of Egypt, but Pharaoh later pursued them to the Red Sea. Moses again believed that God would save them when he declared to the children of Israel:-

> "Fear ye not, stand still, and see the salvation of the Lord, which he will shew to you today: for the Egyptians whom ye have seen today, ye shall see them no more for ever. The LORD shall fight for you, and ye shall hold your peace." (KJV Exodus 14:13-14)

The Lord divided the Red Sea, thereafter, so that the children of Israel could pass through on dry land, but, when the Egyptians tried to pass through, the Lord caused the waters to come together again to destroy the Egyptians (i.e. the enemy was destroyed). The children of Israel were graciously saved by God. They went through a baptism. They left their old life in Egypt and it was buried in the Red Sea. Thereafter, they were to live a life wholly given to God in the Promised Land. Moreover, they physically could not return to their old life in Egypt because the way was blocked off by the Red Sea.

Again, we see the principle of death, burial and resurrection.

God raised up Joshua to lead the children of Israel, thereafter, in the conquest of most of the Promised Land. The vast majority of the children of Israel that had left Egypt wandered in the wilderness for forty years and died. They did not enter into the Promised Land because of unbelief (Hebrews 3:19), so God baptised the next generation that did believe. Prior to the conquering of Jericho, the children of Israel had to cross over the river Jordan (Joshua 3-4). Joshua believed God. God was gracious and the children of Israel passed over the river Jordan on dry land:-

> "Hereby ye shall know that the living God is among you, and that he will without fail drive out from before you the Canaanites, and the Hittites, and the Hivites, and the Perizzites, and the Girgashites, and the Amorites, and the Jebusites. Behold, the ark of the

covenant of the Lord of all the earth passeth over before you into Jordan." (KJV Joshua 3:10-11)

The priests that bore the ark stepped into the river Jordan so that, "the waters of Jordan [were] cut off from the waters that [came] down from above," (KJV Joshua 3:13). Thereafter, the people passed over and the Lord brought the waters together again.

So, from where did the waters of Jordan flow? They flowed from a city called "Adam" (Joshua 3:16). We see a very interesting picture here. The waters of Adam were, "cut off." In a sense, everything that had flowed down from the helpless race of Adam had been cut off by God. The children of Israel could not go back over the river Jordan and return to Egypt. They could not return to their old lives of slavery. They could only press forward, as God led them. Ultimately, they moved forward and they conquered Jericho because God was gracious to them.

This again represents death, burial and resurrection.

In the gospel of Mark, we read that, "John (i.e. John the Baptist) did baptise in the wilderness, and preach the baptism of repentance for the remission of sins" (KJV Mark 1:4). John the Baptist came in the spirit of Elijah, as the voice of one crying in the wilderness, to prepare the way of the Lord and to make His path straight (Isaiah 40:3). We will recall that God used Elijah to turn the hearts of the people back to God (1 Kings 18) and John the Baptist also came in that spirit, only he was preparing the hearts of the people for the coming of the Messiah.

95

God was gracious in sending John the Baptist to prepare the people for the coming of Jesus Christ.

John's baptism was a baptism of repentance for the remission of sins. It prepared the hearts of the people by helping them to confess their sins and to come before God, in humility. John baptised in water, in the river Jordan. The picture was that the person was submerged in the river. They left their sins and their sinful life behind (i.e. they died and they were buried) and when they were raised back up out of the water they gave themselves wholly to God.

This is another revelation of death, burial and resurrection.

In Matthew 3, we see the baptism of Jesus, by John the Baptist, in the river Jordan. Understandably, John was hesitant to baptise Jesus because the Lamb of God had absolutely no sins to confess and had nothing that He needed to repent of. However, on the instruction of Jesus, John graciously relented in order to, "fulfil all righteousness" (KJV Matthew 3:15).

Jesus did not go down into the waters to confess his sins because he had no sins to confess. Some have said that Jesus went down into the waters to identify with the sins of the world, or to pick up the sins of the world, and there may be some truth in that. Ultimately, however, Jesus went down into the waters because it was what His Father in heaven had asked Him to do.

Jesus lived, as a man upon the earth, with His life fully laid down before God. He never raised up 'self' within Him. Going down into the waters of baptism (i.e. into death and burial) was a demonstration, therefore, of a life fully laid down before God. What was the result? Jesus came back up out of the water, at perfect peace with God. The Spirit of God descended and lighted upon Him and His Father in Heaven declared, "This is my beloved Son, in whom I am well pleased" (KJV Matthew 3:17).

God had used Elijah, in his day, to turn the hearts of His kingdom people back to Him. John the Baptist came in the spirit of Elijah and prepared the hearts of the people to receive the King of the kingdom. The King and the kingdom had come and all righteousness was fulfilled.

God was not simply gracious in sending His Son. The very grace of God had come.

This all foreshadowed the death, burial and resurrection of Jesus.

John the Baptist baptised in water and, as we read the scriptures, we know that this baptism was given to him from heaven (Luke 20:1-8). However, John the Baptist knew that a greater baptism was to come:-

> "I indeed baptise you with water unto repentance: but He that cometh after me is mightier than I (i.e. Jesus Christ), whose shoes I am not worthy to bear, He shall baptise you with the Holy Ghost and with fire: whose fan is in His hand, and He will thoroughly purge His floor, and gather His wheat into the garner, but He will burn up the chaff with unquenchable fire." (KJV Matthew 3:11-12)

Jesus Christ did come. He lived, as a man upon the earth, with His life fully laid down before God. He

97

had been baptised in water, but He said that, "I have a baptism to be baptised with; and now I am straitened till it be accomplished" (KJV Luke 12:50). He was, of course, talking about the cross and He set His face like a flint to go through it.

Jesus laid down His life upon the cross for the sins of the whole world. He died and was buried and God the Father raised Him up from among the dead. Salvation has been won for us by the grace of God and by the faith of our Lord Jesus Christ. Jesus explained to His disciples that, if they wanted to enter into this salvation, they would also have to go through the same baptism that He went through (Mark 10:39).

That baptism is death, burial and resurrection.

When we are convicted (or convinced) of our sins by the Holy Spirit and turn to God, in humility (i.e. we repent), we put our faith in Christ and in the finished work of salvation that He accomplished on the cross (i.e. we exercise our own faith to believe). We are declared 'just' (i.e. we are justified), simply because we have believed into the Son of God. The judgment of God passes over us because we are cleansed and purged by the blood of the Lamb of God. We are crucified with Christ and are buried with Him. Our old life is gone and we cannot return to it. It is no longer we who live. Rather, we are filled with the Holy Spirit and the life of Christ is birthed within us. The resurrected life of Christ is in us, therefore, and God the Father is also in us. God is no longer simply gracious to us. The grace of God is within us. The life of God, in Christ, is at work in us, willing and doing of His own good pleasure.

This is what it means to be born again. This is Christ's baptism. This is baptism in the Holy Spirit. It is death, burial and resurrection. The Holy Spirit comes and burns away all that is not of God (i.e. the chaff of our old life that surrounds the grain of wheat) so that the grain of wheat (i.e. Christ within us) is revealed. This is Christ revealed in His saints upon the earth.

This is the one true baptism to which all the others point.

We see then, in the New Covenant era (i.e. after Pentecost), that people believed and, thereafter, they were baptised. Sometimes the head of the house believed and was baptised and the whole household with him. Some believe that this refers to infant baptism, but faith precedes baptism. The more natural interpretation would then be that the head of the household believed and so did the whole household. The head of the house and the whole household, therefore, were baptised.

In any event, this should not distract us.

We also see examples in the New Testament of people believing, being baptised with water and, thereafter, receiving the Holy Spirit. Conversely, we see people believing, receiving the Holy Spirit and, thereafter, being baptised in water. The difference in the order of events should not trouble us. God calls us all from different situations. Moreover, each of us have probably heard and understood the gospel in slightly different ways because the fullness of the gospel is not universally preached. We should not, therefore, hold overly strong views regarding the order of things. The important thing is that the spiritual reality to which water baptism points has actually occurred.

However, what is the water baptism that is practiced in the churches today?

Certainly the vast majority of Christian denominations would say that water baptism does not save us and that is true. Water baptism is simply symbolic of being baptised with the Holy Spirit. Either, we believe, give ourselves wholly to God, receive the Holy Spirit and are baptised in water as a testimony to the fact that the Holy Spirit has already come, or we believe, give ourselves wholly to God and are baptised in water in the expectation of receiving the Holy Spirit.

Jesus told His disciples to, "Go ye therefore, and teach all nations, baptising them in the name of the Father, and of the Son, and of the Holy Ghost" (KJV Matthew 28:19). Why then, after Pentecost, did the Apostle Peter declare that people should, "Repent, and be baptised every one of you in the name of Jesus Christ for the remission of sins, and ye shall receive the gift of the Holy Ghost"? (KJV Acts 2:38). This should not trouble anyone:-

> "For it pleased the Father that in Him (i.e. in Jesus Christ) should all fullness dwell (i.e. the fullness of God); and, having made peace through the blood of His cross, by Him to reconcile all things unto Himself, by Him, I say, whether they be things in earth, or things in heaven." (KJV Colossians 1:19)

The fullness of God dwells in Jesus Christ. It is correct, therefore, to baptise in the name of Jesus Christ. It is also correct to baptise in the name of the Father, the Son and the Holy Spirit. They are One and the same.

We also do well to remember that:-

"There is one body (i.e. the body of Christ, the Church), and one Spirit (i.e. the Holy Spirit), even as ye are called in one hope of your calling; one Lord (i.e. Jesus Christ), one faith (i.e. the faith of Christ), one baptism (i.e. the baptism of the Holy Spirit), one God and Father of all, who is above all, and through all, and in you all." (KJV Ephesians 4:4-6)

Finally, as an aside, I should also say that part of the symbolism of water baptism is that water washes. Some may say that the water is symbolic of washing away our sins and I can sympathise with that. However, it required the blood of animals in the Old Covenant to cover sins and it required the blood of Christ in the New Covenant to atone for sins and to destroy the very power of sin.

Jesus explained to His disciples, "ye are clean through the word which I have spoken unto you" (KJV John 15:3) and they were to abide in His word. This is what was promised through the prophet Ezekiel when God said, "Then will I sprinkle clean water upon you, and ye shall be clean" (KJV Ezekiel 36:25). The reference here is to the Word of God, as, "Faith cometh by hearing, and hearing by the word of God" (KJV Romans 10:17).

This is the Word become flesh. This is the man, Jesus Christ.

After the crucifixion of Christ, "one of the soldiers with a spear pierced His side, and forthwith came there out blood and water" (KJV John 19:34).

101

"This is He that came by water and blood, even Jesus Christ; not by water only, but by water and blood. And it is the Spirit that beareth witness, because the Spirit is truth" (KJV 1 John 5:6). "There are three that bear witness in earth, the Spirit, and the water, and the blood: and these three agree in one" (KJV 1 John 5:8).

The waters that cleanse, therefore, are the very words of Jesus Christ, which are spirit and life (John 6:63).

Is it any wonder that the Word of God became flesh, therefore, and washed the feet of the disciples as a demonstration of these things?

'There And Back Again'

The principle of death, burial and resurrection is paramount to New Covenant Salvation. Once you begin to understand this, even in principle, if not in reality, you cannot help but to see that it pervades the scriptures here, there and everywhere.

One such picture of this, in scripture, can be seen with Elijah and Elisha in 2 Kings 2.

Elijah was a prophet in the northern kingdom of Israel during the reigns of King Ahab and King Ahaziah. The name Elijah means 'God is Jehovah', or 'Yahweh is my God' and God performed many mighty miracles through Elijah. Arguably, the greatest of those miracles was when God answered by fire and the heart of the people was turned away from Baal and turned back to the one true God (1 Kings 18).

[If you wish to read everything about Elijah, in context, then I would encourage you to read all of 1 Kings and the first two chapters of 2 Kings.]

When we pick up the story of Elijah in 2 Kings 2, we quickly learn that Elijah's time upon the earth was drawing to a close and that God was going to take Elijah up into heaven by a whirlwind. However, Elijah first had to journey from Bethel, then to Jericho and then to the river Jordan. At that time, Elisha was already a companion to Elijah and Elisha was insistent upon following Elijah wherever he went.

Elijah had learned the cost of following God in his own day. He knew that the life of a true prophet of God was not an easy task. Absolutely everything had to be given over to God. This may explain, in part, why

Elijah attempted to dissuade Elisha from following him, but Elisha was absolutely insistent upon following Elijah at every turn.

Elijah and Elisha arrived at the town of Bethel. The name Bethel means 'House of God'. The sons of the prophets were at Bethel (and, subsequently, they were also at Jericho) and they enquired of Elisha if he already knew that God was going to take Elijah away. Elisha answered in the affirmative.

I will begin my narrative from this point.

Elijah began his journey at Bethel, the House of God. This house was obviously on earth. Our Lord Jesus Christ also began His journey from the House of God, but His journey commenced from the House of God that is in heaven. Jesus Christ came to the earth and, ultimately, He became the House of God and the testimony of God upon the earth.

Elijah proceeded to the city of Jericho. Historically, Jericho was a place of testing. Joshua and the children of Israel, in their day, believed God. They crossed the river Jordan on dry land and conquered the city of Jericho (i.e. the enemy) by the grace of God. Our Lord Jesus Christ, having come from heaven, was also tested by Satan after He had fasted in the wilderness for forty days. He was tested, He believed, and He also conquered the enemy.

Elijah then proceeded to the river Jordan. He took off his mantle and struck the waters of the river Jordan, so that they divided, and he crossed over on dry land. This is reminiscent of Moses crossing the Red Sea, with the children of Israel, and of Joshua subsequently crossing the river Jordan, with another generation of the children of Israel. This is a picture of judgment and of

104

baptism, whereby Elijah went down into death and burial. Similarly, our Lord Jesus Christ became sin and was judged for the sins of the whole world upon the cross. This was the baptism that He had to go through. His baptism was also one of death and burial.

When he was on the other side of the river Jordan, Elijah asked Elisha what he could do for Elisha before he departed. Elisha asked for a double portion of the spirit that was in Elijah and Elijah explained that that was a difficult thing.

As Elijah and Elisha walked on, a chariot of fire and horses of fire parted Elijah and Elisha and Elijah went up by a whirlwind into heaven. Having gone through death and burial (in picture form), Elijah was now brought up into heaven (which is a picture of resurrection). Likewise, having gone through death on the cross and subsequent burial, our Lord Jesus Christ was declared to be the Son of God with power when God the Father raised Him from among the dead and seated Jesus at His right hand in heaven.

[Please note that I am absolutely not saying that Elijah is an Old Testament picture of our Lord Jesus Christ. I am simply identifying parallels that allude to baptism and the principle of death, burial and resurrection. The spirit of Elijah is, of course, more closely identified with John the Baptist.]

Elijah had completed his course upon the earth and God took him up to heaven. Similarly, our Lord Jesus Christ completed all that His Father in heaven had commanded Him to do upon the earth and, thereafter, He took Jesus up to heaven.

Elisha then took up the mantle of Elijah. In faith, he asked, "Where is the LORD God of Elijah?" (KJV 2

Kings 14). When Elisha struck the waters of the river Jordan with the mantle of Elijah, the waters parted and Elisha crossed back over the river Jordan on dry land.

Elisha had received a double portion of the spirit of Elijah and he subsequently performed twice as many miracles as Elijah. Our Lord Jesus Christ received the Holy Spirit without measure. After He was glorified in heaven, He poured out the Holy Spirit into His saints (i.e. into the Church), having told His disciples that they would do greater works than Him (i.e. all the works of God can now be done through the various saints in the body of Christ all over the world, rather than the works of God being done through one man).

We do not receive a portion of the Spirit, but rather a measure of the fullness of the Spirit. We also cross the river Jordan, in a sense. When we receive the Holy Spirit we go down into death and burial so that the resurrected life of our Lord Jesus Christ is raised up in us.

Elisha then journeyed back to Jericho and the sons of the prophets judged that the same spirit that had been in Elijah was now in Elisha. Elisha also healed the waters at Jericho so that there would not be any more death in the land, thereafter, and so that the land would not be barren. Elisha proved that he had the same spirit as Elijah. Similarly, as saints in the Church of our Lord Jesus Christ, our faith is tested. If we do not show forth the fruits of the Holy Spirit will others see that we have the same Spirit as our Lord Jesus Christ? Will others see the life of Christ in us? Have we sufficiently died to self so that Christ is clearly revealed in us?

That is the test that we face in our Jericho.

It is a trying and a testing of our faith, which should produce pure gold within us. If Christ has been manifested within us, "a well of water springing up into everlasting life," (KJV John 4:14) will be within us and it will overflow into the dead and barren souls of those around us (i.e. it will produce waters in the wilderness and streams in the desert, as described in Isaiah 43:18-21).

Finally, Elisha returned to Bethel, the House of God. It was here that Elisha was mocked by a group of forty-two children. Elisha cursed the children and God sent two female bears out of the wood to tear the children. The Church of Jesus Christ is the House of God and the testimony of Christ upon the earth (i.e. the life of God, in Christ, in us). We are the temple of the living God upon the earth, therefore, and, if the Church is showing forth the life of Christ to the earth, then others will be drawn to Christ. However, the world is full of mockers and those that persist in mocking the saints of God and rejecting God will, ultimately, be judged.

Moreover, whenever we begin to enter fully into this so great salvation that Christ has won for us, we may find that people in the various church denominations may also mock us because we no longer fit into their particular moulds. We may also find that, just as our Lord Jesus Christ was rejected by the religious leaders of His day, so, too, we may be rejected and ridiculed and mocked by the religious leaders of our day.

This should by no means surprise us.

However, having entered into Christ Jesus, we must ever, "press toward the mark for the prize of the high (or upward) calling of God in Christ Jesus" (KJV Philippians 3:14).

We must follow our Lord Jesus Christ rather than man and, akin to Elisha, we must be absolutely insistent upon doing so.

'The King James Version'

I am not a 'King James Only' supporter of scripture. Although I use the King James translation of scripture in my daily readings and study, I also refer to other translations, such as the New American Standard Bible, the English Standard Version and the New International Version.

The King James Version (also known as the Authorised Version) is written in older English and some of the language in it is truly beautiful, but sometimes it can be difficult to understand. Sometimes it even becomes necessary to consult a dictionary when reading it.

Some archaic words and terms in the King James Version can also appear to be a little peculiar in our day and age. It can be useful to read modern translations of scripture, therefore, in order to see their various interpretations.

However, there is one thing that I absolutely lament in many of the newer translations of scripture. So far as I can see, very few (if any) of the new translations refer to the "faith of Christ" (e.g. in Galatians 2:16, Galatians 2:20, Romans 3:22, or Philippians 3:9), though many other (usually older) translations, such as the King James Version, Young's Literal Translation, the Berean Literal Bible, the International Standard Version, the Net Bible, the Aramaic Bible in Plain English and the Darby Bible Translation (among others) do refer to the "faith of Christ" (i.e. Christ's own faith) and not simply to our own "faith in Christ" (i.e. our ability to believe in Jesus Christ and the salvation that He has won for us).

I am not an expert in the Greek language. I simply know that most modern translations of scripture refer to our "faith in Christ" in Galatians 2:16, Galatians 2:20, Romans 3:22 and Philippians 3:9, rather than the "faith of Christ". I am convinced, in my own mind, as to which interpretation correctly expounds the gospel in all of its fullness, but I would encourage anyone who is intrigued by the different translations to research the matter for themselves.

As I said in the foreword to this book, certain truths of the gospel may have been watered down, or are in danger of being lost altogether. It would be a travesty if the knowledge of the "faith of Christ" and the fullness of the gospel, therefore, were to be lost.

If we do not believe in the fullness of salvation, we cannot expect to enter into the fullness of salvation.

Printed in Great Britain
by Amazon

41781337R00066